'This timely book will help one ~~a~~ the Holy Spirit . . . what pleases Him. I heartily recommend this book which can help every Christian experience tremendous peace and calm as they adjust to the Holy Spirit – our Senior Partner.'
Dr David Yonggi Cho, Church Growth International

'This is the most important book I have read for a long time. I have been challenged by insights I have never seen before. The truths continue to haunt me.'
Lyndon Bowring, Executive Director, CARE

'This book is unique, timely and very much needed.'
Colin Dye, Senior Minister, Kensington Temple

'If your sensitivity to the Spirit is confined to worship meetings, this book is not for you. But if you see the Spirit, given as a gift for the whole of life including both home and work, this book will open your eyes and your hearts to God's sensitivity and your future effectiveness.'
Gerald Coates, Team Leader, Pioneer

'Here he is again putting the cat amongst the pigeons – this time with his concept of "pigeon religion". If he's right it is too scary for words; let us hope he's wrong.'
Rob Parsons, Care for the Family

'Essential reading for any leader or minister. It could save their ministry.'
Alex Buchanan, author and minister-at-large

Also by R. T. Kendall

The Anointing: Yesterday, Today, Tomorrow
The Gift of Giving
The Thorn in the Flesh
Worshipping God

The Sensitivity
of the Spirit

The Forgotten Anointing

R. T. Kendall

Hodder & Stoughton
LONDON SYDNEY AUCKLAND

First published in Great Britain in 2000

The right of R.T. Kendall to be identified as the Author of
the Work has been asserted by him in accordance
with the Copyright, Designs and Patents Act 1988.

10 9 8 7 6 5 4 3

British Library Cataloguing in Publication Data
A record for this book is available from the British Library

ISBN 0 340 75628 4

Typeset by Avon Dataset Ltd, Bidford-on-Avon, Warks

Printed and bound in Great Britain by
The Guernsey Press Co. Ltd, Channel Isles

Hodder & Stoughton
A Division of Hodder Headline Ltd
338 Euston Road
London NW1 3BH

To Bob and Diane

Contents

Foreword

I have known and loved R.T. for about twelve years now, and I am privileged to be one of his friends. I believe that he is an important man in today's Church. We need his grasp of theology and his openness to the Holy Spirit in our day when there is so much shoddy theology, abuse of the Holy Spirit and subtle heresy about.

His openness to the moving of the Holy Spirit and to those who are gifted by the Spirit causes him to put his reputation on the line by allowing those preachers in his pulpit who would be regarded as dangerous by many other ministers. However, his passion for the Word of God enables him to keep the balance between the Word and the Spirit, and his discernment enables him to guard the pulpit from mere heretics. Praise God for that!

R.T.'s desire for God comes through very clearly in his writings and this saves him from becoming a 'dry as dust' theologian. This is a major reason why God blesses him and his ministry, and overrules the mistakes that he is honest enough to admit to.

The book will show that the Holy Spirit is God. Not a thing, nor an influence. He is co-equal with God the Father and God the Son. He has deep and passionate feelings. He is not merely touchy, but he can be deeply grieved by our insensitivity to him. He cannot be whistled up when we want our meetings to be exciting. He is not only around to put us on the floor, or make us laugh. He does both very well, but he is out to convict us of sin and to lead us into holiness, too.

One of the greatest dangers we can fall into is that of substituting our ideas for the Spirit's agenda and therefore engaging in work that God never initiated. How grieved he is when we try to work without him! R.T. rightly says, 'When the Holy Spirit is grieved the anointing lifts.' Who wants that? We need to be as sensitive as we can to him so that he only has to whisper when we need a course correction in our ministry or meetings. After all, at the judgment seat of Christ there are no rewards for uncommanded work. The book addresses the need to remember the sensitivity of the Holy Spirit and our need to be sensitive to him. To allow him to direct our lives and ministries as he sees fit.

R.T.'s previous book on anointing, which highlights the danger of losing it, healthily frightened me – this present book healthily scares the life out of me. (Or is it *into* me?) But I need its message. My greatest fear through the years is that I may fail on my last lap by grieving the Spirit. God grant that I won't. My fear of God used to centre mainly on his punishment; that remains to some extent, but now my main fear of God is the fear of grieving him by forgetting his sensitivity. This book helps me to remain mindful of it. It is essential reading for any leader or minister who desires to retain the anointing on his work. It could save our ministry.

Many of us forget the extreme sensitivity of the Spirit, and we need faithful friends to remind us of it. By writing this book, R.T. is such a friend.

Alex Buchanan
Burnham
November 1999

Preface

This book is the product of at least four episodes in my life over many years. The first is a sermon preached by Joe Jones, my first roommate at Trevecca Nazarene College in Nashville, Tennessee. I heard him preach a sermon which he called 'The Lost Christ', based upon Luke 2:41–2. This is the first time I gave any thought to this passage.

The second event was hearing Dr Hywel Jones read John 1:32–3 in Westminster Chapel. He happened to be in the service and I asked him if he would read the Scripture I would be preaching from. Either it was his Welsh accent or the Spirit of God (I think the latter), but the way he pronounced 'remain' went so deep in me that I thought about it for many, many days. I don't believe there have been many times in my life when the mere reading of Scripture has had such a profound impact upon me. This book would not have been written had not Hywel read John 1:32–3 as he did.

The third development was when I addressed a group of Elim ministers in Northern Ireland earlier this year. I gave some talks based upon *The Anointing: Yesterday, Today, Tomorrow*. One of the ministers, the Rev. Walker Gorman, approached me to say, 'I have a story that fits with what you have been teaching and I think it could interest you.' It was the account of Sandy and Bernice, which begins Chapter 1. I cannot imagine this book without that amazing story. Thank you, Walker.

Finally, only three months ago my wife Louise and I visited Pete and Melissa Cantrell in Ada, Oklahoma. What I learned from Pete about doves and pigeons has given this book such a flavour that I hate to think how impoverished it would be without this information. Talk about providence! Thank you, Pete!

I therefore believe that I have been prepared to write what follows for quite a long time. I only pray that it will bless you and bring honour and glory to the name of our Lord Jesus Christ.

My thanks to my new editor, David Moloney of Hodder and Stoughton, who has been a delight. My thanks to a host of friends, especially Lyndon Bowring, Colin Dye and Rob Parsons for their suggestions. Thanks also to Anne Williams, who read my manuscript.

When I thought of who might do the Foreword I asked myself, 'Who will understand this book more than anybody in Britain?' I suspect it takes a line not frequently considered by preachers and theologians. I kept thinking of Alex Buchanan. Before I asked him to write the Foreword I merely asked him to read the manuscript and give me a hard critical feed-back. His response was exactly as I had hoped and I then asked him to write the Foreword, which he has kindly done. I express my love to Alex and Peggy.

This book is dedicated to Bob and Diane Ferguson who now reside in Mandeville, Louisiana. They have been the dearest of friends for over twenty-five years. A book dedicated to them is long overdue. God bless you, Bob and Diane.

R. T. Kendall
November 1999

Every year his parents went to Jerusalem for the Feast of the Passover. When he was twelve years old, they went up to the Feast, according to the custom. After the Feast was over, while his parents were returning home, the boy Jesus stayed behind in Jerusalem, but they were unaware of it. Thinking he was in their company, they travelled on for a day. Then they began looking for him among their relatives and friends. When they did not find him, they went back to Jerusalem to look for him. After three days they found him in the temple courts, sitting among the teachers, listening to them and asking them questions. Everyone who heard him was amazed at his understanding and his answers. When his parents saw him, they were astonished. His mother said to him, 'Son, why have you treated us like this? Your father and I have been anxiously searching for you.' 'Why were you searching for me?' he asked. 'Didn't you know I had to be in my Father's house?' But they did not understand what he was saying to them. Then he went down to Nazareth with them and was obedient to them. But his mother treasured all these things in her heart. And Jesus grew in wisdom and stature, and in favour with God and men. (Luke 2:41–52)

Introduction

My greatest fear is that God would remove his hand from me.
(Billy Graham)

I was converted when I was six – on April 5th 1942. I began studying the Bible earnestly in my teens, and felt called to the preaching ministry when I was nineteen. In over fifty years of studying the Bible there is a truth that has alarmed me more than any other. You might think it has to do with standing before God at the Final Judgment. But, surprising as it may seem, it isn't that. It is the possibility of grieving or quenching the Holy Spirit without knowing it: the painless way in which the anointing can be lifted from me. When this occurs I know nothing whatever at first but carry on as though nothing has happened.

There are two passages from the Bible, one from each testament, that illustrate what I mean:

Then she called, 'Samson, the Philistines are upon you!' He awoke from his sleep and thought, 'I'll go out as before and shake myself free.' But he did not know that the LORD had left him. (Judg. 16:20)

> After the Feast was over, while his parents were
> returning home, the boy Jesus stayed behind in
> Jerusalem, but they were unaware of it. Thinking he
> was in their company, they travelled on for a day.
> Then they began looking for him among their
> relatives and friends. (Luke 2:43–4)

These passages show that the special presence of God can be withdrawn and yet the people who have been experiencing that same presence feel nothing when it happens. This shows the painless way I can lose the anointing. I can displease the Lord and feel nothing. It even demonstrates the very real possibility that I could spend years doing what I presumed was God's will – preaching, teaching, witnessing and being involved in church work – when God was hardly in it at all. I may also have the applause and respect of people the whole time and they not have a clue I have moved ahead of Jesus.

One of the mysteries of the anointing is that one can be unaware of it when it is working most powerfully and, on the other hand, not be conscious should it be lifted. When Moses came down from Mount Sinai, he was 'not aware that his face was radiant' (Exod. 34:29). But Samson, who could tear a lion apart with his bare hands 'as he might have torn a young goat' (Judg. 14:6), was as weak as a kitten when the anointing left him, but was unconscious of this until he tried to do what had seemed so natural the day before. For the supernatural often seems natural to the anointed man or woman.

This book is taking the things I said in *The Anointing: Yesterday, Today, Tomorrow* a step further. For one thing, as long as we are conscious of the special presence of God, we can be sure we are not yesterday's men or women. But the main thing is that we develop a sensitivity *to* the Spirit because we are aware of the sensitivity *of* the Spirit. This is one of the paramount things God was teaching David – a type of 'tomorrow's man or woman' – as he waited for his time to come.

The anointing is the power of the Holy Spirit – the special presence of God. And yet the anointing can be manifested in any number of ways. It is important to remember this in the light of John's use of this word. First, 'But you have an anointing from the Holy One, and all of you know the truth' (1 John 2:20). Second, 'As for you, the anointing you received from him remains in you, and you do not need anyone to teach you. But as his anointing teaches you about all things and as that anointing is real, not counterfeit – just as it has taught you, remain in him' (1 John 2:27). These verses refer to the presence of the Holy Spirit that is in every believer (cf. Rom. 8:9). Every Christian therefore has an anointing. But this is sovereignly applied by the Spirit 'as he determines' (1 Cor. 12:11). Therefore not every Christian has the same specific application of the anointing; we are all different.

Samson's anointing manifested itself in unusual physical strength. Once when the Philistines bound Samson with two new ropes, 'The Spirit of the LORD came upon him in power. The ropes on his arms became like charred flax, and the bindings dropped from his hands. Finding a fresh jawbone of a donkey, he grabbed it and struck down a thousand men' (Judg. 15:14–15).

Samson, however, had a particular weakness and it had to do with women. He fell in love with Delilah – a set-up by the Philistines. They used her to get to know the secret of his great strength. He finally told her everything: 'If my head were shaved, my strength would leave me, and I would become as weak as any other man' (Judg. 16:17). While he was asleep she had his head shaved. 'His strength left him' (Judg. 16:19).

> Then she called, 'Samson, the Philistines are upon you!' He awoke from his sleep and thought, 'I'll go out as before and shake myself free.' *But he did not know that the LORD had left him.* (Judg. 16:20)

Samson therefore felt nothing at the time. He only discovered the loss of his strength when it was too late. 'Then the Philistines seized him, gouged out his eyes and took him down to Gaza. Binding him with bronze shackles, they set him to grinding in the prison' (Judg. 16:21).

For all I know there may have been an unconscious diminishing of Samson's anointing during the time he foolishly allowed Delilah to keep probing him for his secret. 'With such nagging she prodded him day after day until he was tired to death' (Judg. 16:16). What we do know is that when his head was shaved his strength utterly left him. The main thing, however, was that he lost the anointing and didn't know it. At first.

There have been servants of Christ – some with high profile – who apparently felt no loss of anointing at the time when they compromised themselves. Since they were used so powerfully – which they often took as proof of God's approval and of the anointing – they sometimes felt nothing when they gave in to sexual temptation. Billy Graham also says that it seems the devil gets 75 per cent of God's best servants through sexual temptation.

The account of Samson is an Old Testament example of what the apostle Paul calls grieving the Spirit: 'And do not grieve the Holy Spirit of God, with whom you were sealed for the day of redemption' (Eph. 4:30). When the Holy Spirit is grieved the anointing lifts. We usually feel nothing at the time. It is some time later we notice that we carried on by habit or the momentum of a natural gift. It means we can lose the special presence of God – what we should want most – and that is what happened to Samson. The lifting of the anointing was thus unconscious and painless.

I now turn to the biblical story that has mainly inspired me to write this book: the account of Joseph and Mary moving ahead of Jesus and leaving him behind in Jerusalem (Luke 2:41–52). Although this refers to Jesus rather than the Spirit, he is nonetheless to be seen here as a way in which the sovereign Holy Spirit may test our sensitivity to him by not moving with us just because we choose to carry on. The occasion was not only the observance of the Feast of the Passover, but it was also Jesus' bar mitzvah. This is when a Jewish boy is recognised formally as becoming a man. Although from birth Jesus was God as though he were not man and man as though he were not God, Jesus was now truly authenticated as the God-man, certainly by Joseph and Mary, who knew the facts.

There are theological implications here that have to do with when Jesus was truly conscious of who he was and what his mission was – no doubt fully realised at his baptism (Matt. 3:17). But suffice it to say that on this occasion, as John Calvin put it, Jesus was given a single 'practice round' of what he would develop into. There was the twelve-year-old Jesus, sitting among the teachers like a rabbi, astonishing all who heard him by his understanding, questions and answers. What a moment it must have been.

But Joseph and Mary missed it all at the time. This was apparently going on for three days – all without their knowledge. I fancy that when we get to Heaven we will see a video replay of the whole three days! All this was happening because God was sovereignly at work. Jesus was doing his Father's business. It was a 'practice round' of what he would later say about himself: 'I tell you the truth, the Son can do nothing by himself; he can do only what he sees his Father doing, because whatever the Father does the Son also does.' (John 5:19). Or as he would also put it, 'By myself I can do nothing; I judge only as I hear, and my judgment is just, for I seek not to please myself but him who sent me' (John 5:30). What a pity that Joseph and Mary missed it.

The scenario turns largely on one striking phrase: '*Thinking he was in their company*, they travelled on for a day' (Luke 2:44). When the Feast was over Joseph and Mary returned home. However, Jesus stayed behind but 'they were unaware of it'. In other words, they sincerely thought Jesus was right there with them. Why? They presumed he would adjust to them. After all, it was – as far as they were concerned – time to go home. They did not see a need of adjusting to him. But he chose to stay behind.

This reminds me of the words of the Episcopal rector who shocked many Christians by his comment on a national radio broadcast: 'If the Holy Spirit were totally withdrawn from the Church today, 90 per cent of the work of the Church would go on as if nothing had happened.' And this can happen to you or me as well as the Church.

That is what Joseph and Mary did, moving on as if nothing had happened. Jesus stayed behind, but they were 'unaware' of it. They sincerely thought he was with them.

Joseph and Mary went to the Feast of the Passover every year. They no doubt attended other annual Feasts as well, since they wanted to be obedient to the Law (Luke 2:39). This probably means they sang the Psalms of Ascent (Ps. 120–134) with the pilgrims as they ascended the holy hill of Jerusalem. They knew the territory well.

Luke's account, which he no doubt learned from Mary (Luke 2:51), is our only information about Jesus between the accounts of his miraculous birth and his public appearance on the scene at the age of thirty (Luke 3:23). We all would love to know more, but we must conclude that God has given us all we need.

But why did Luke include this account of Joseph and Mary taking the twelve-year-old Jesus to Jerusalem? There are far more reasons than I will attempt to give, but I believe that one of them is what partly inspires the theme of this book. Why is this event important for us?

- It shows how we can run ahead of God as a result of not focusing on his Son and adjusting to the sensitivity of the Spirit. We, like Joseph and Mary, may think the whole time that Jesus is with us, only to discover that he is hardly with us at all. We therefore must adjust to him and not expect him to adjust to us.
- The immediate presence of Jesus is like the anointing, the immediate and direct witness of the Spirit of God. This therefore shows one of the differences between God's omnipresence and his special presence. Theologians often speak of the attributes of God, three of which are the Big O's: his omnipotence

(he is all-powerful), his omniscience (he knows everything), and his omnipresence (he is everywhere). Indeed, listen to the psalmist:

'Where can I go from your Spirit?
Where can I flee from your presence?
If I go up to the heavens, you are there;
    if I make my bed in the depths, you are there.
If I rise on the wings of the dawn,
    if I settle on the far side of the sea,
even there your hand will guide me,
    your right hand will hold me fast'

(Ps. 139:7–10)

Therefore it is quite wrong in one sense to say that God is not with us. After all, God said, 'Never will I leave you; never will I forsake you' (Heb. 13:5). But there is also the *special* presence of God – the anointing – which we can lose. That is what happened to Joseph and Mary. It happened to Samson. However, God had not totally left Samson. 'The hair on his head began to grow again after it had been shaved' (Judg. 16:22), and he got his anointing back in the end (Judg. 16:30).

- If we discover that we have moved ahead of God, and have left him behind, we must go looking for him. That is what Joseph and Mary had to do. 'When they did not find him, they went back to Jerusalem to look for him' (Luke 2:45).
- Once we have lost God's special presence, we can only find him by initially returning to the place where we lost him. By 'place', I do not necessarily

10

mean a literal, physical place – as in a building or even a geographical location. I mean (1) recalling what it was like when he was consciously present; (2) remembering the circumstances that may have contributed to his staying behind; and (3) reassessing and repenting of the self-justifying (but ill-advised) ways we proceeded, thinking he was in our company. We find him eventually by discovering where he is and coming to terms with what he is doing. Joseph and Mary had to go back to Jerusalem – where they lost Jesus, where they finally found him and saw what he was up to.

- This account demonstrates that it is easier to lose the anointing than it is to get it back. After a day's journey Joseph and Mary realised they had left Jerusalem without Jesus. It was another three days before they found him. 'After three days they found him in the temple courts, sitting among the teachers, listening to them and asking them questions' (Luke 2:46).

- We miss seeing the next sphere of God's activity when we move on without him. He does not promise to adjust to us. He carries on without us, but he still continues to work. 'My Father is always at his work ... and I, too, am working' (John 5:17). It is a sober reminder that Heaven doesn't shut down merely because we ourselves are not directly involved. Joseph and Mary could not conceive of Jesus doing anything extraordinary without them, but he did. 'Didn't you know that I had to be in my Father's house?' (Luke 2:49) he said to them.

All this began because once the Feast was over, Jesus chose

to stay behind and his parents headed for Nazareth without him. Had Jesus not stayed behind – or had Joseph and Mary remained with him – Luke would not have had this story to tell. But because of two things, Jesus staying behind in Jerusalem and his parents heading for home without him, we can learn a lot about God's sovereignty and human responsibility.

I believe the Bible categorically affirms the sovereign grace of God in salvation. This means that we are chosen apart from works (2 Tim. 1:9), saved apart from works (Eph. 2:8–9) and kept apart from works (Rom. 8:28–39). We are loved with an everlasting love (Jer. 31:3). This means that there is nothing we can do to make God love us more and nothing we can do to cause him to love us less. In a word: we are secure and kept by the sheer grace of God.

But that is not all we need to know when it comes to living the Christian life and pleasing God. God puts us on our honour to guard the 'good deposit that was entrusted' to us. This is done 'with the help of the Holy Spirit who lives in us' (2 Tim. 1:14). That deposit is the anointing, the special presence of God. This we can lose without forfeiting being saved. God takes the responsibility for our making it to Heaven but warns us that the anointing is a trust here below that must be carefully guarded by us with the help of the Spirit.

I write this book to examine ways by which we may hope to avoid the mistake Joseph and Mary made. What they did by moving on without Jesus seems understandable to any parent. Mary probably felt embarrassed. She knew in her heart that they had not been as careful as they should have been. So I write this book to see if we can discover hints from this account that will show us how not to move ahead without the Lord. It is a mistake I myself have made hundreds of times.

We don't know, of course, all of the reasons Jesus stayed behind in Jerusalem without telling his parents. But I suspect it was mainly for what he was called to do, but partly for them as well. We also don't know all the facts as to why Joseph and Mary headed for Galilee without their son. It certainly seemed inevitable at that time. But it almost always does seem unavoidable at first when it comes to grieving or quenching the Spirit.

I therefore do not write this book with the view that we can reach the place this side of Heaven that we will never again move ahead of the Holy Spirit. I don't want to be too hard on Joseph and Mary, or too hard on myself; neither do I want you to feel any false guilt if you too see yourself in what Joseph and Mary did. After all, 'If we claim to be without sin, we deceive ourselves and the truth is not in us' (1 John 1:8). We all need the rebuke of Ecclesiastes 7:16 from time to time, 'Do not be over-righteous, neither be overwise – why destroy yourself?' As Solomon put it, 'There is no one who does not sin' (2 Chr. 6:36). Simon Peter honestly thought he loved the Lord Jesus more than the others did. And he was the very one who denied knowing Jesus when the pressure was on (Matt. 26:69–75). At the end of the day, we are going to cause the Heavenly Dove to fly away from time to time. Nobody's perfect. As Calvin put it, 'In every saint there is something reprehensible.' Is not this part of the meaning of the psalmist's words, 'To all perfection I see a limit' (Ps. 119:96)?

I must therefore bring in an extremely important caution. There may be a person with an 'over-sensitive' conscience who might carry this principle too far – and find himself or herself in an unnecessary bondage. For example, some people may be so fearful of grieving the Spirit that they are afraid to do *anything* without a minute-by-minute sense of clear guidance. They worry about which pair of shoes to wear, which tie to put on or whether to read a newspaper. They cannot turn on the television without 'guidance'. They are fearful of any entertainment, fearful of laughing at a joke or spending money in a good restaurant. The irony is, such a bondage equally grieves the Spirit! For where the Spirit of the Lord is, there is liberty (2 Cor. 3:17). One legacy of the Reformation is the doctrine of Christian liberty. 'It is for freedom that Christ has set us free. Stand firm, then, and do not let yourselves be burdened again by a yoke of slavery' (Gal. 5:1).

A healthy fear of grieving the Spirit should not lead you to be afraid to enjoy life to the full, to laugh uproariously with friends or to make common-sense decisions day and night. God is not unreasonable. His commands are never 'burdensome' (1 John 5:3). Bondage to rules is not what this book is about.

On the other hand, I must eagerly desire all of God I can possibly have. I would love it if God would increase my anointing each day I live. I therefore want to learn ways by which I can adjust to the special presence of God.

Moving ahead without the Lord is an easy thing to do. We've all done it. But we miss what God is doing elsewhere while we are, as it were, on our way to Galilee. I think it would not happen were we to adjust to the Dove, which I will now explain.

1

The sensitivity of the Heavenly Dove

The voice of the turtle is heard in the land. (S. of S. 2:12 AV)

A few years ago a British couple, Sandy and Bernice, accepted a call from their denomination to be missionaries in Israel. A house was provided for them near Jerusalem. After they moved into their new home they noticed that a dove had come to live in the eaves of the house. They were honoured to be living near Jerusalem and were particularly thrilled to have the dove come and live there. They considered it to be something of a seal of approval from the Lord, a confirmation that they were in the right place.

Sandy noticed an unsettling pattern in the dove's behaviour, however. Every time a door slammed shut, or if there was a lot of noise in the house or they raised their voices, the dove would be disturbed and flutter off, and sometimes it would not return for a good while. This worried Sandy as he felt they were in danger of frightening the dove off permanently. With this in mind, he brought up the matter with his wife.

'Have you noticed that every time there is a lot of noise, or if we slam the door, the dove flies away?' he asked.

'Yes, and it makes me feel sad, and I am afraid the dove will fly away and never come back.'

'Well,' said Sandy, 'either the dove will adjust his behaviour to us or, if we really want to make sure we never lose him, we will have to adjust our behaviour to the dove.'

Watching that dove was a daily reminder to that precious couple. It changed their lives for ever.

When Jesus was baptised he saw the Holy Spirit 'descending like a dove and lighting on him' (Matt. 3:16). John the Baptist saw this as well. For John gave this testimony:

> I saw the Spirit come down from heaven as a dove
> and *remain* on him. I would not have known him,
> except that the one who sent me to baptise with
> water told me, 'The man on whom you see the
> Spirit come down and *remain* is he who will baptise
> with the Holy Spirit.' (John 1:32–3)

The more I have learned about the person of the Holy Spirit, and the nature of a turtle-dove, the more extraordinary I find this account. First, it is unusual – probably unprecedented – for a dove like this ever to alight voluntarily on a human being. But for the dove to *remain* is quite astonishing indeed. I don't know if our Heavenly Father chose the dove as one of the first symbols in the New Testament for the Holy Spirit because of John the Baptist's familiarity with doves. I only know that the dove coming down and remaining on Jesus told John all he needed to know at the time; 'that this is the Son of God' (John 1:34).

An important word obviously is 'remain'. The Holy Spirit

remained on Jesus. The Holy Spirit comes on me from time to time but I'm afraid that sometimes he doesn't stay long. Dr Martyn Lloyd-Jones was fond of quoting one of the Puritans who said: 'The Holy Spirit comes by foot but leaves by horseback.' This shows how sensitive the Holy Spirit is and how easy it is to grieve him. However, when he does come down, his conscious presence is wonderful. There is no more peaceful, blissful moment than when the Heavenly Dove descends on me. But why doesn't it last? There is not only peace when the Dove is present, but also presence of mind. Clear thinking. Courage and confidence. A feeling that God is in complete control. No need to panic, not even a fear of panic. 'No fear of bad news' (Ps. 112:7). It is almost impossible to describe, but one verse of the hymn 'Like a river glorious' comes close:

> Hidden in the hollow of his blessed hand,
> Never foe can follow, never traitor stand;
> Not a surge of worry, not a shade of care,
> Not a blast of hurry touch the spirit there.
>
> (Frances Ridley Havergal, 1836–79)

The dove, especially the turtle-dove, is apparently a very shy, even hypersensitive bird. You can feed the pigeons in Trafalgar Square, but probably not a turtle-dove. I doubt a dove like that ever comes near Trafalgar Square. Although pigeons and doves both belong to the same order of birds, namely the *columbi-formes*, the Bible apparently makes a distinction between pigeons and doves (Lev. 12:8). Scientifically the turtle-dove belongs to the genus *Streptopelia turtur*. Either, however, was acceptable for sacrifice. Which of these Joseph and Mary brought is not known (see Luke

2:24). In much the same way, a lamb or goat was acceptable (Lev. 3:1); they look very alike in many ways, yet they are different.

The Bible does not say that the Spirit came down from heaven as a pigeon. There would probably have been nothing unusual about a pigeon descending on an individual. Or even remaining.

Shortly after we moved to England in 1973, we came into London to feed the pigeons in Trafalgar Square. I have a photograph of our son T.R. when he was seven, with four pigeons on each arm and one on his head! It would seem that such is out of the question when it comes to a turtle-dove. We now live in central London. Every spring we have to come up with a new method to get rid of the pigeons which perch by our bedroom window, making guttural noises that wake us up too early in the morning. Louise has tried opening the window, shooing them away with a mop or broom handle. But these pigeons seem impervious to any punishment we can administer to them. They are a terrible nuisance.

I decided to do some investigating on pigeons and doves. Despite what the encyclopaedias say, I knew there must be *some* differences – at least in temperament – between pigeons and doves. But I did not have the evidence or experience to prove it. Moreover, I was quite certain that Sandy and Bernice would not scare a pigeon away with a slammed door or heated argument inside. A pigeon – at least the pigeons of Trafalgar Square – would adjust to nearly any situation, but almost certainly a turtle-dove would not.

An unexpected invitation came our way while we were in America in August 1999. Our old and dear friend Pete Cantrell from Oklahoma, whom I happened to quote in

The Anointing: Yesterday, Today, Tomorrow ('The greatest free-dom is having nothing to prove'), arranged for me to preach where he goes to church in Ada, Oklahoma. After Louise and I arrived Pete wanted to show me his pigeons! I had not known until then that he has raised pigeons and turtle-doves all his life. Pete is a Cherokee Indian and inherited a love for doves. His middle name is Grayson, after the Grayson dove.

I couldn't believe it! I told him virtually everything I have written above, and that I was confused over the supposed similarity between pigeons and doves. I have talked with some of the top experts on doves and pigeons on both sides of the Atlantic, and they all insist that there is virtually no difference between pigeons and doves – unless, however, it is the turtle-dove. There are many kinds of pigeons and many kinds of doves, but, says Pete Cantrell, the turtle-dove is different. First, Pete said, 'I sometimes question whether they should be in the same family because of the homing instinct. A pigeon has a homing instinct – a turtle-dove has none.' Pete was speaking out of fifty years of experience in raising doves and pigeons, and observing them carefully.[1] He made the following observations:

- Turtle-doves never fight; pigeons fight with each other all the time. 'Turtle-doves I raise are always peaceful and quiet. Their soft cooing is very beautiful and reassuring. Pigeons are belligerent, noisy and anything but tranquil.'
- Turtle-doves can't stand noise; pigeons don't mind noise.
- Turtle-doves are afraid of humans; pigeons aren't afraid of people.

- Turtle-doves are not territorial, that is, defensive for a particular location; pigeons are very territorial and will even bully one another for a special place to perch.
- Turtle-doves cannot be trained or domesticated; pigeons, having a homing instinct, can be trained. 'I could put a red box in the centre of New York City and train a pigeon to come to that box,' said Pete.
- Turtle-doves let out of a cage will never return unless there is no other source of food. 'I once released fifty white turtle-doves, thinking they would at least return for food. Not one came back. Friends phoned from all over Ada saying, "Some of your doves are in our back yard." ' I watched Pete let a dozen pigeons out of their cage. They soared. As soon as he called to them they returned to him at once. This helps explain the dove Noah sent out from the ark: 'But the dove could find no place to set its feet because there was water over all the surface of the earth; so it returned to Noah in the ark. He reached out his hand and took the dove and brought it back to himself in the ark' (Gen. 8:9). The dove returned a second time with an olive leaf but when the waters receded the dove 'did not return to him' (Gen. 8:11–12).
- A turtle-dove will mate with only one other dove. 'Doves mate for life,' says Pete, 'but pigeons will sometimes have more than one mate.'

Finally, Pete added, 'A pigeon could never be the symbol of the Holy Spirit. Can you imagine a love song or a poem about the loud boisterous pigeon?'

Any analogy can be pressed too far, and there is a danger

of oversimplification in these illustrations and comparisons between pigeons and doves. For there are many kinds of pigeons, many kinds of doves and there is more than one kind of turtle-dove. I do not wish to enter into a controversy with anyone! I do, however, believe that there are some visible and temperamental differences between the pigeons[2] most of us know as pigeons and the turtle-dove, which is likely to be the dove symbolising the Holy Spirit.[3]

When I was a student at Southern Baptist Theological Seminary in Louisville, Kentucky, I took a course in archae-ology which included a trip to Israel. One day as I walked towards the Western Wall (known as the 'Wailing Wall') an Israeli explained to me that once in a while you see a dove perched in one of the crevices of the Wall. I thought I was being privileged to see such a sight! I took a photograph and included it as part of my research project. But my balloon was punctured. My professor gently asked me to take another look. To my chagrin, it was not a dove, but a pigeon! Perhaps a dove occasionally visits the Wailing Wall. But not that day. Long seen as a symbol of peace, the harmless and gentle dove had already been designated by God as a symbol of the Holy Spirit. Jesus described a dove as 'innocent' (Matt. 10:16; 'harmless' AV), which comes from the Greek *akeraios*. It is a word which the ancients understood as 'pure' or moral innocence: that which is in its original state of intactness. The turtle-dove, which thrives in the Middle East, would probably have been the dove of which the Bible speaks. A fruit of the Spirit is 'gentleness' (Gal. 5:23). Paul urged, 'Let your gentleness be evident to all' (Phil. 4:5). The wisdom that is 'from above is first pure, then peaceable, gentle, and easy to be entreated' (Jas. 3:17 AV). That is what *we* are like when the Heavenly Dove is present.

I will never forget how humbled and embarrassed I was that I had not noticed that this was but a *pigeon* I had photographed at the Western Wall in Jerusalem. The suggestion the Israeli made about a dove preconditioned my thinking. It had not crossed my mind that it could be a pigeon! The power of suggestion shaped my expectancy to such an extent that I thought I had pulled off a real coup for my research project.

This has made me wonder how often many of us may have confused a dove with pigeons at a spiritual level. We may hastily assume that the Dove has come, but a more objective examination might just show that it was a pigeon! This has given me a new phrase – 'pigeon religion'. The same evening that Pete Cantrell explained the differences between turtle-doves and pigeons he turned on the TV to a religious programme. I had watched it occasionally during the summer. I listened to the claims. I watched the gifted TV preacher pump the viewing audiences for financial support, telling them why this particular ministry was 'anointed' and deserved support. I pray I am not being insensitive to the Holy Spirit, but I fear that so much today that purports to be the presence of the Spirit is but pigeon religion.

It is my view that the genuine presence of the Holy Spirit is not as common as we may want to believe. It is also my fear that many of us have run slip-shod over this matter and have forgotten that the Holy Spirit is a very, very sensitive person.

I know that I have been very guilty in this area. I have joined in conversations with those who appear to feel no great anguish when speaking disparagingly of others. We all claim to want God's blessing on us – and even take strong public stands for the truth! But a real conscientiousness with regard to grieving the Spirit by attitudes and words seems absent. It is as if we think our official positions or titles exempt us from having to watch what we say. The sober truth is, God will not bend the rules for any of us, whatever our position may be.

It seems to me that this is a neglected emphasis in our theology and talk about the Holy Spirit. If I am correct, it would explain the lack of real power in our churches and in our personal lives. What if, when we get to Heaven and look back on all our claims to the power of God, we learn that it was not the Dove among us at all but one who looks so much like the Dove?

The dove is not the only symbol of the Holy Spirit in the Bible, and, as I said, any analogy or comparison can be taken too far. However, I write this book not only to try and fill a gap long overdue in our knowledge of the Holy Spirit but also because I think there may be a *link* between the dove and other symbols of the Spirit, such as fire, water, oil and wind. If the New Testament links Jesus with the dove remaining upon him, what does this have to say to us? What is our identity as Christians? If we are truly to be like Jesus (Phil. 2:5ff), is it not right to want to imitate him in this way as well? If I am to be today's man or tomorrow's man – and make sure I am not yesterday's man – should I not want to ensure my anointing by focusing on the sensitivity of the Spirit as well as the wind and fire?

This surely means we must respect the Spirit as a person of dignity and honour, and want to know him – as opposed to using him for my own goals. Of course I want the fire.

23

O God of burning, cleansing flame:
Send the fire!
Your blood-bought gift today we claim:
Send the fire today!
Look down and see this waiting host,
And send the promised Holy Ghost;
We need another Pentecost!
Send the fire today!
(William Booth, 1829–1912)

Yes, we long to experience the fire as well as a mighty rushing wind in our church. But I believe that the way to power and more anointing is by being more sensitive to the Holy Spirit. I suspect that the Dove is the link to the fire.

The word 'sensitivity' has two meanings: getting one's feelings hurt, and being careful not to hurt another's feelings. The former often suggests a weakness in one's personality. We may have to 'walk on eggshells' with some people who are easily upset. The latter, being sensitive to another's feelings, is a strength. We all need to develop in this area. Therefore the matter of sensitivity has two meanings. And yet when we speak of the sensitivity of the Holy Spirit we must refer to *both* of these meanings. We may or may not think this is a very attractive quality in the Holy Spirit's personality. But, like it or not, the Holy Spirit is like a turtle-dove – and flutters away where peace does not prevail. However, the Holy Spirit is equally sensitive to *our* feelings. The Holy Spirit is a gentleman.

There are two main truths I want this book to make clear. First, the sensitivity *of* the Holy Spirit. This refers to his passive feelings. It refers to how sensitive he is when he is grieved. It is what causes the Dove to fly away. If we can tune in to the sensitivity of the Spirit, we learn what grieves him, how to avoid grieving him and how we must adjust to him if we want his intimate company.

Second, developing a sensitivity *to* the Spirit. This refers to his active will, or voice. If we develop a sensitivity to the Spirit we will hear him when he speaks and avoid quenching the Spirit. That way we can see the glory of God manifested in our lives and, hopefully, in the Church.

The apostle Paul says, therefore, 'And do not grieve the Holy Spirit of God, with whom you were sealed for the day of redemption' (Eph. 4:30). This means that the Holy Spirit has feelings and that he can get his feelings hurt. As I said, that is the way he is. The Greek word translated 'grieve' (*lupeo*) comes from *lupee*, which means 'pain' or 'sorrow'. It is the opposite of joy.

The Holy Spirit is a person. We must never make the mistake of calling him 'it'. He is the third person of the Godhead, Jesus being the second person (John 1:1). This does not mean that either the Son or the Spirit is less in deity than the Father; it is at best a human way of attempting to understand the three persons of the Trinity. The Holy Spirit is a person as Jesus is a person. As a person, Jesus therefore had a personality. The disciples knew the sound of his voice, the colour of his skin, hair and eyes; they knew how tall he was and exactly what he looked like. They would have known what his personality was like. One thing is certain: because he had the Spirit without limit (John 4:34), he would have perfectly manifested all of the fruits of the Spirit.

That the Holy Spirit descended and *remained* on Jesus tells us as much about Jesus as it does about the Holy Spirit.

The Holy Spirit was at home with Jesus. They were mutually adjusted to each other. There was no bitterness or hate, no grudges, panic or spirit of vindictiveness. 'Gentle and humble in heart' (Matt. 11:29), Jesus did not quarrel or cry out; a bruised reed he would not break (Matt. 12:20). Moreover, it was far more than what Jesus actually *said* that gripped the temple guards who suddenly changed their minds about arresting him; it was an anointing that lay behind and accompanied his words. ' "No one ever spoke the way this man does," the guards declared' (John 7:46).

What can we learn about the Holy Spirit's personality? For one thing, he and Jesus had much in common, in that neither the Son nor the Spirit spoke on his own. Jesus said he could do 'only what he sees his Father doing' (John 5:19). Likewise Jesus said that the Holy Spirit would 'not speak on his own; he will speak only what he hears' (John 16:13). As the Holy Spirit could be grieved, there is every reason to believe that Jesus too was very sensitive – but did not always show it outwardly. We know from the apostle Paul that the Holy Spirit can also be quenched. Paul's words, 'Do not put out the Spirit's fire' (1 Thess. 5:19) come from the Greek *abennumi* which basically means 'to quench'. In the ancient Greek world it referred mostly to fire or burning objects: that is, to extinguish fire. The Holy Spirit was therefore seen not only as a dove but also as what seemed to be 'tongues of fire' (Acts 2:3). The warning not to quench the Spirit can only mean that sometimes the Spirit's fire can be put out. This quenching was possibly implicit when Jesus refused to perform miracles in Capernaum 'because of their lack of faith' (Matt. 13:58).

It is hard to know the difference between the Holy Spirit being grieved and being quenched. But part of the difference is that his being grieved refers to the Spirit not being allowed to be himself – what he could be *in us*. His being quenched refers to his not being allowed to *do* what he could do through us. When he is *ungrieved* in us we will manifest his personality, called 'fruits of the Spirit': namely, love, joy, peace, patience, kindness, goodness, faithfulness, gentleness and self-control (Gal. 5:22ff). This means we will be like Jesus. When he is *unquenched* in us we may well manifest his power, perhaps also as in the gifts of the Spirit (1 Cor. 12:10–12). There is no doubt that the capabilities of being grieved and being quenched overlap and that this distinction too should not be pressed too far. For they are similar in some ways. I suspect there has been a tendency for some, however, to be more concerned with quenching the Spirit, when there is a desire to see his power – like signs and wonders – than grieving the Spirit, which in some ways focuses more on Christ-likeness. Sadly, there has been a disproportionate interest in the gifts of the Spirit among some Christians. For some of us seem to want power more than purity, signs and wonders more than gentleness and graciousness: the forgotten anointing.

The anointing must be the totality of all that the Spirit is and is able to do. We must therefore want to exemplify the personality of Jesus as much as to demonstrate his power. And it seems to me that we must begin from within, that is, experiencing the Holy Spirit in us *ungrieved* in our private lives before we can anticipate an outward demonstration of his power. This order is one that God is not tied to, for he can sovereignly overrule any of us whenever he wants to. But in order to expect the dove of the Spirit to *remain* it is surely essential that all we *are* does nothing to cause the Dove to flutter away.

I fear that the neglect of this aspect of the Holy Spirit's personality has resulted in the Church's tendency to move on without Jesus, thinking the whole time that he is with us in a special manner when he is not. We have taken him for granted. It seems not to have crossed our minds that he as a person has a dignity of his own; he wants to be consulted, honoured and *recognised* before we proceed.

What is needed, then, is a sensitivity to the Spirit. It means a sensitivity to his ways and – may it please God – to an immediate awareness of his *absence*, should he withdraw to any degree. How quickly we recognise his absence is probably a fairly good test as to how well acquainted we are with him. 'They have not known my ways,' said an offended Holy Spirit.

So, as the Holy Spirit says:
'Today, if you hear his voice,
do not harden your hearts
as you did in the rebellion,
during the time of testing in the desert,
where your fathers tested and tried me
and for forty years saw what I did.
That is why I was angry with that generation,
and I said, "Their hearts are always going astray,
and *they have not known my ways.*"
So I declared on oath in my anger,
"They shall never enter my rest." ' (Heb. 3:7–11)

But does not this teaching make the Holy Spirit vulnerable to the charge of being capricious? Under no circumstances. He may appear that way from our point of view. But God always has a reason for what he does. He promised Moses,

'I will have mercy on whom I will have mercy, and I will have compassion on whom I will have compassion' (Exod. 33:19). The Holy Spirit always mirrors the unity of the Godhead. Even though 'the wind blows wherever it pleases', Jesus' reference to the Spirit (John 3:8), the Spirit never does anything 'on his own' (John 16:13). He therefore reflects the will of the Father. The psalmist spoke of the *second* person of the Trinity, 'Kiss the Son, lest he be angry and you be destroyed in your way, for *his wrath can flare up in a moment.* Blessed are all who take refuge in him' (Ps. 2:12). The Holy Spirit likewise can be grieved suddenly – but never without reason. We therefore must lower our voices and adjust to him if it is the anointing we want. This is partly what is meant by knowing his 'ways'.

I almost blush to admit that I was in the ministry for many years before this aspect of the Holy Spirit began to influence me. I had a 'sound' doctrine of the Holy Spirit, but I fear it was largely soteriological: that is, it had to do mainly with applying the teaching of salvation. In other words, my doctrine of the Spirit was chiefly understood as the Holy Spirit *applying* the Gospel. For if the Holy Spirit does not apply the good news that Jesus paid our debt on the cross, no one will be converted. Jesus too had a sound soteriological doctrine of the Holy Spirit and proved that by saying, 'No one can come to me unless the Father who sent me draws him' (John 6:44). Only the Holy Spirit opens people's eyes and hearts.

But I began to recall my experience of driving in my car one Monday morning – on October 31st 1955 – on my way to Trevecca Nazarene College in Nashville, Tennessee. I have described this in *The Anointing: Yesterday, Today, Tomorrow.* I will only say here that the glory of the Lord filled the car; my heart, mind and life were instantaneously changed. This came as an immediate and direct manifestation of the Spirit. It was not a case of the Gospel merely being applied; the Holy Spirit came in very clearly and noticeably as well. It was *so* powerful. The person of Jesus was literally more real to me than anybody around me. However, this glow of experience began to diminish in time.

Years later, my weekly visits to Dr Martyn Lloyd-Jones at his home in Ealing from 1977 to 1981 gave me a hunger and thirst to experience again the precious intimacy of God's presence. I used to talk about it with him. Sound doctrine simply wasn't enough; I wanted more. It was during those days I first sensed how easy it was to grieve the Spirit. I would try so hard to get it right! I began to pray more. But if any, even in my family, for example, would disturb me when I was praying I would become very annoyed. Instead of God being impressed at my efforts, the thanks I got was that the Dove fluttered away. Never mind that I was trying to please God; he would not bend the rules for me even if my motive was to keep from grieving him. I have learned countless times: the Dove will not adjust to me, I must adjust to him. And I have to add: it isn't easy.

I would go so far as to say that the easiest thing in the world to do is to grieve the Holy Spirit. This is partly because any anger, grudge or resentment comes so naturally. When Paul spoke of the possibility of grieving the Spirit in Ephesians 4:30, the very next thing he said was:

> Get rid of all bitterness, rage and anger, brawling
> and slander, along with every form of malice. Be
> kind and compassionate to one another, forgiving

each other, just as in Christ God forgave you.
(Eph. 4:31–2)

At the head of the list, then, is bitterness. Bitterness, or resentment, is one of the chief ways we grieve the Holy Spirit. Sadly, resentment always seems right at the time. Furthermore, we often do not realise *at the time* that we grieve the Spirit. He quietly flutters away with no announcement or fanfare. You just realise some time later that he's gone, whether it was bitterness or something else that drove him away. As we have seen, Samson told the closely guarded secret of his strength to Delilah, but 'he did not know that the Lord had left him' (Judg. 16:20). But when the Spirit departs like this, it doesn't mean we have lost our salvation. For Paul said, 'And do not grieve the Holy Spirit of God, with whom you were *sealed* for the day of redemption' (Eph. 4:30). Nothing could be clearer than that! Samson himself got his old anointing back in the end and accomplished more 'when he died than while he lived' (Judg. 16:30). Bitterness is therefore not the only way we can grieve the Spirit, but it is at the top of Paul's list in Ephesians 4:31ff. However, the list continues, and sexual immorality is mentioned in Ephesians 5:3.

A chief strategy of Satan is to get us to grieve the Spirit, whether by sexual immorality or a bitter attitude. The devil knows God's ways. And ours. After all, as Jonathan Edwards said, he was trained in the best Divinity School ever – the heaven of heavens. When we grieve the Spirit we force God to treat us like an enemy (Jas. 4:4). That is exactly what Satan wants. If he can cause us to grieve the Spirit – working through any weakness we may have – he wins a battle. It is the way Satan worked in ancient Israel; through the influence of Balaam and Balak Israel began to sin and consequently incurred God's wrath (Rev. 2:14). For this reason the devil, who knows each of us backwards and forwards, watches day and night for an opportunity to lure us to grieve the Spirit.

I referred above to losing that sense of the intimate presence of God. I can't be sure that there was not a gradual if not unconscious diminishing of the sense of his presence, but I do remember how I became aware that I had completely lost this intimacy. It was in August 1956. I had always thought, and still think, I have the best and most godly dad in the world. But I was not prepared for his reaction to my 'Damascus road' experience. Not that he objected to the experience; he was unhappy with the theology it led me to, which did not cohere with the doctrines of my old denomination. In my efforts to explain, I lost it. I can never forget how distraught I was and, most of all, the realisation later that the Dove had completely flown away. It is easier to lose the anointing than it is to get it back.

I started on a pilgrimage many years ago to recover that old sense of the ungrieved Spirit powerfully inside me. It has returned in slow stages. This is partly because the way back must be a return *to* the anointing, not a return *of* the anointing. As we will see below, we must move on and be willing not to have everything exactly as we once knew it. Someone once put it this way: you can step out of a flowing stream but you can never step back in at the same place. Seldom is everything exactly as it once was; we must adjust to what God has for us now – not then. It seems to me that at some point in the summer of 1956 the Lord Jesus must have 'stayed behind' but I was initially unaware of it – like Joseph and Mary (Luke 2:43). I kept on going, thinking he was in my company. At first I did not want to admit I had lost something, that is, the special anointing. But I eventually came to terms with the truth. Little was the same as before. I looked in my comfort zone to find what I lost, but with no joy. Like Joseph and Mary, I have had to go back to my equivalent of Jerusalem. It has been a long journey, but one worth travelling. This, too, is what this book is about.

2

Adjusting to the Heavenly Dove

Return, O holy Dove! Return,
Sweet messenger of rest!
I hate the sins that made Thee mourn
And drove Thee from my breast.
(William Cowper, 1731–1800)

Sandy and Bernice's lives were dramatically altered overnight for one reason: the company of an earthly dove meant so much to them. They made a conscious, deliberate choice to adjust to it, and their lives were never the same again. How much more important, do you suppose, is the company of the Heavenly Dove in our lives, whose personality is far more sensitive than an earthly dove? Your own life too can be wonderfully altered overnight – and you too will never be the same – if you consciously and deliberately choose to adjust to the Dove. He will manifest himself in surprising ways. The consequences are incalculable.

But why won't the Dove adjust to us? The truth is, he could – if he wanted to. The proof of this is the way God dealt with Jonah after Nineveh was not destroyed. Jonah had put his reputation on the line: 'Forty more days and Nineveh will be overturned' (Jonah 3:4). The people repented. 'When God saw what they did and how they turned from their evil ways, he had compassion and did not bring upon them the destruction he had threatened' (Jonah 3:10). This should have pleased any man of God, but not Jonah. He was 'greatly displeased and became angry' (Jonah 4:1). That was sufficient to drive the Dove away. 'But the LORD replied, "Have you any right to be angry?"' (Jonah 4:4). This shows that despite Jonah's resentment, God maintained communion with him. But God still explained his actions with the worm and the vine. And yet the truth is, God has been gracious like that to all of us at times. 'For he knows how we are formed, he remembers that we are dust' (Ps. 103:14).

Generally speaking, however, God tends to call the Dove away from us when we are filled with bitterness, hold grudges, refuse to forgive, or do not have our sexual appetite under control. He requires us to adjust to the Dove, which means adjusting to the sovereignty and standard of the gentle Spirit.

It is always God's sovereign prerogative to determine what happens next. Jesus deliberately 'stayed behind' (Luke 2:43). But his parents failed to discover this. Jonathan Edwards taught us that the task of every generation is to discover in which direction the Sovereign Redeemer is moving, then to move in that direction. This, then, is how Joseph and Mary missed what the Lord was up to. Jesus stayed behind in Jerusalem, 'but they were not aware of it'.

They no doubt felt that if Jesus made an important decision, they would be the first to be told. After all, they *were* special; they, if anyone, would be informed of what God would do next!

Adjusting to the Dove must be done often without our

knowing *why* the Spirit is leading in a particular manner. When the angel told Philip to head towards the desert (Acts 8:26), he had no idea why at the time. This shows a highly developed sensitivity to God's voice. It was not a case of Philip being spoken to through the written word or being gripped by a sermon. God spoke to him immediately and directly. Why doesn't this sort of thing happen today? It should. After all, as Dr Lloyd-Jones used to say, the Bible was not given to replace direct revelation; it was given to correct abuses. By abuses he meant going against Scripture – God's final and ultimate revelation. But many of us are so loath to listen to God speaking immediately and directly that there are seldom abuses (mistakes we can make) to correct! Should God be pleased to speak in such a manner, it would also mean that much is going on behind the scenes – in the heavenlies. He trusts us to obey without our knowing all of the reasons why he gives a particular word. In the same way, then, Jesus stayed behind in Jerusalem and did not explain the reason to his parents.

If we want God to speak directly to us today as he did to Philip, it follows that we will want the honour that comes from God alone and not that which comes from people (John 5:44). This may include keeping quiet about such immediate and direct communication from God. For this sort of thing could easily go to our heads. That is probably why God doesn't dispense such intimacy very widely. But it is something he would do with us if we could keep to ourselves such two-way communication with him (Ps. 25:14).

There is a lot implied when it comes to God's honour. We must be willing to appear foolish and stupid to ourselves and to others by obeying God's immediate voice. This also means that we must be vulnerable to criticism and being corrected. The criticism may be just or unjust. If it is unjust, we must show a sweet spirit. If it is a fair criticism, we must accept correction. Defensiveness against valid criticism grieves the Spirit; it shows resentment. Maintaining a teachable spirit and a graciousness towards our critics will help ensure that the Dove remains.

I suspect that staying behind was no small decision for Jesus himself to make. As this was the first 'practice round' of what he would develop into, perhaps it was also the first crucial test in Jesus' life of whether he would listen exclusively to his Father. He too would need to develop a sensitivity to the Spirit. For it was undoubtedly the Father's beckoning that led Jesus to stay in Jerusalem. It was therefore a real test of Jesus' obedience. He learned obedience through suffering (Heb. 5:8) and part of the suffering is always to put God first rather than those closest to us.

It must therefore have been very difficult for the boy Jesus. Some twenty years later he would say, in response to being told, 'Your mother and brothers are outside looking for you' (Mark 3:32), 'Here are my mother and my brothers! Whoever does God's will is my brother and sister and mother' (Mark 3:34–5). For all I know that may not have been easy for him to say, even twenty years on. But imagine the twelve-year-old Jesus having to stay behind and listen only to his Father God.

Sometimes it is God's will for us just to *stay*. We may want to move on; God sometimes wants us to stay. We may say, 'It's time to get moving – let's get the show on the road.' God says, 'Stay.' 'In quietness and trust is your strength' (Isa. 30:15). We may be bored. 'The Feast is over, let's go home,' Joseph and Mary were saying. God told his Son, 'Stay behind.'

This is a lesson that the ancient people of Israel had to learn. They took their cue only from the visible glory of God: the pillar of fire by night and the cloud by day.

> In all the travels of the Israelites, whenever the cloud lifted from above the tabernacle, they would set out; but *if the cloud did not lift, they did not set out* – until the day it lifted. So the cloud of the LORD was over the tabernacle by day, and fire was in the cloud by night, in the sight of all the house of Israel during all their travels. (Exod. 40:36–8)

Israel was locked into this manner of direct guidance from God. They could only move when the cloud lifted. If the cloud did not lift, they stayed. No matter how tedious and tasteless that particular place in the wilderness might have been, they had to 'stay put' until they were released to move on. The cloud did not adjust to the Israelites; they had to adjust to the cloud.

It often takes as much courage to stay as it does to move. It may take even more faith sometimes to remain where you are than to explore a new geographical area. It may not be mere boredom, however, that tempts one to move on; sometimes it is opposition. Paul went into Corinth to preach the Gospel. His custom was to offer the Gospel to Jews first (Rom. 1:16). This he did in Corinth. 'But when the Jews opposed Paul and became abusive, he shook out his clothes in protest and said to them, "Your blood be on your own heads! I am clear of my responsibility. From now on I will go to the Gentiles" ' (Acts 18:6). Paul left the synagogue where he had been preaching and went next door. He had some spectacular conversions (Acts 18:7–8), but the persecution was so fierce that Paul *wanted* to move on. 'One night the Lord spoke to Paul in a vision: "Do not be afraid; keep on speaking, do not be silent. For I am with you, and no one is going to attack and harm you, because I have many people in this city" ' (Acts 18:9–10). The consequence was that Paul stayed for a year and a half. A great church was formed and we all have the benefit of 1 and 2 Corinthians as a result. All because Paul stayed.

Whenever God says, 'Stay,' it is with a definite purpose. We will never be sorry when we remain where we are if God says we must. We may not know the reasons at the time. I am hearing more and more of people leaving secular work for Christian work. They assume the new sphere will be 'spiritual'. In fact, a young man recently rang a friend of mine and said, 'I can't wait to get out of my office and get into Christian work. I'm so tired of office politics.' My friend, who has spent many years in a para-church organisation, couldn't stop laughing for a month.

Perhaps Jesus didn't know entirely why he was constrained to remain behind when Joseph and Mary were moving on. But he adjusted to the Father's will in any case.

Louise and I came to England in 1973 for me to do research at Oxford. T.R. was seven, Melissa was three. We initially agreed to stay for two years, the minimum stay then required by Oxford University to get a research degree. Those were hard days. I felt out of my depth from the first day. Here I was in that august seat of learning, coming from the hills of Kentucky – a state not known for its high educational standards. And here I was trying to adjust to the British system, to which nearly all around me were well acquainted. On top of that, our children struggled with their school and relationships. Many days T.R. would come home crying, asking, 'How long will we be staying over here?' I assured him – not long. 'One day we are going home.' The two years at Oxford had to be extended to three, then another three months. It was during those last three months that I was invited to preach at Westminster Chapel. Our ministry began in February 1977. In May 1977 we were called to stay permanently. One of the hardest things I ever had to do was to look T.R. in the eyes when he said, 'Daddy, you said we were going home.' That was nearly twenty-three years ago, as I write these lines. I still feel the pain to this day. The cloud has refused to lift after all those years. But God's sovereign prerogative to stay is never without its reason – or benefits.

Jesus' staying behind was partly because he had more to learn in Jerusalem – and to teach others as well. He amazed the teachers of the Law with his questions and answers. It was a way of learning for Jesus. Dr Michael Eaton reckons that the twelve-year-old Jesus was zealous to discover everything he could about God and his will. 'Although Jesus was the Son of God, he was also a genuine man,' as Michael puts it. 'He did not know everything all in one instant. He had to learn and grow. So he took every opportunity to learn more of the things of God.'

The day would come that, possibly, some of these very teachers, or certainly men like them, would be Jesus' chief antagonists. This time with them enabled Jesus to see what they were like, how their minds worked. There was probably no hostility at this time, but rather a friendly atmosphere. The teachers were only fascinated that a twelve-year-old Jewish boy could hold their attention. But it was preparation

41

for Jesus. He would very likely mull over their questions and answers, how they viewed the Law and what their messianic expectations were. It would be another eighteen years before he would be confronted by the likes of them, but during this time he could reflect on *all* that had happened during those days in the temple courts. Sadly, it would be teachers of the Law who helped lead the way to his death years later (Luke 23:10).

This may have been training for Jesus to learn to *listen*. Luke says he was among the teachers 'listening to them' (Luke 2:46). Listening is an art. Few people truly learn to listen. We love to talk more than to listen. I know I do. I find listening hard. A good listener, like a wise judge, listens to all the evidence before making a decision. A doctor who makes a diagnosis before hearing the patient's whole story is not a good doctor. Jesus turned out to be the greatest listener that ever was. He still listens. He is our great High Priest who is able to sympathise with our weaknesses (Heb. 4:15), because he listens.

This may also have been preparation for Jesus asking the right questions. He was not only listening to the teachers in the temple but also 'asking them questions' (Luke 2:46). To ask the right questions reflects acute discernment and wisdom. Years later Jesus would manifest an unparalleled brilliance in asking questions. 'Which is easier: to say, "Your sins are forgiven," or to say, "Get up and walk"?' (Luke 5:23). Or how does one answer this question: 'What good is it for a man to gain the whole world, yet forfeit his soul?' (Mark 8:36)? He could initiate a discussion by raising questions that showed the folly of his opponents' views.

While the Pharisees were gathered together, Jesus asked them, 'What do you think about the Christ? Whose son is he?' 'The son of David,' they replied. He said to them, 'How is it then that David, speaking by the Spirit, calls him "Lord"? For he says, "The Lord said to my Lord: 'Sit at my right hand until I put your enemies under your feet.' " If then David calls him "Lord", how can he be his son?' No one could say a word in reply, and from that day on no one dared to ask him any more questions. (Matt. 22:41–6)

As staying behind in Jerusalem was a test of Jesus' obedience to the Father then, so his mind being shaped during those three days prepared the way for his being the great Teacher one day. Jesus grew mentally, physically, spiritually and socially. For Luke says Jesus grew 'in wisdom and stature, and in favour with God and men' (Luke 2:52).

Sadly, Joseph and Mary forfeited the privilege of seeing how some of these aspects of Jesus' life developed. For they wanted to move on. They were miles down the road towards Galilee and would not know what was going on – where it mattered. The real sphere of God's influence and power remained precisely where they had just been!

And yet it is equally God's sovereign prerogative some-times to be *silent*. For the question may be asked, 'Why didn't Jesus *explain* to his mother that he needed to stay behind in Jerusalem?' I think the only answer is, he wasn't allowed to do so. There is 'a time to be silent' (Eccles. 3:7). It takes faith to stay and even more faith to say nothing.

God obviously does not tell us all he knows. He doesn't tell us all we'd love to know. In precisely the same way that this rare account of Jesus' life between his birth and public ministry is *all we need to know*, so does God tell us what we too *need* to know – and *when* we need to know it.

So Jesus was silent regarding communicating to his parents that he must remain behind in Jerusalem. No explanation. No apology. He stayed behind in Jerusalem, but his parents were unaware of it.

Sometimes those of us who think we should be at the head of the queue in receiving a word from the Lord – as if by special privilege – are the last to know. Sometimes people with a prophetic gift feel they must maintain their reputation by *always* having a word. Because they have been singularly used in the past they presume they will continue to be on the front line in revealing to their generation what God is going to do next!

If Jesus could withhold communication from his own parents, God can certainly keep silent regarding any of us. I think a lot of 'prophetic jealousy' exists among those who have a reputation for being gifted with a word of knowledge, or prophecy. You've heard of professional jealousy – it exists with doctors and lawyers. Have you heard of prophetic jealousy? It's worse! I have little doubt that a rival spirit – not a word from the Lord – is what leads some people to take their stand against what God may be up to in a given time. People who are known for their prophetic gift sometimes put themselves under pressure always to have 'a word from the Lord'. The people expect it. Their followers take it for granted. But if someone other than themselves has a word that doesn't include them – or confirm them – they are often ungracious. 'It can't be from God,' they say, 'or I would know.'

God was powerfully at work in Jerusalem. Jesus was the

centre of it all. But his own parents – those who knew him best – weren't in on it. It should be a lesson to you and me. God can use me yesterday, but remain silent today. He can use me today, but speak through someone else tomorrow. It may be someone nobody has heard of that he uses. It may be someone everybody has heard of – but doesn't particularly like – that he uses. For God is sovereign.

This was almost certainly the first time Jesus would be 'sitting among the teachers'. Sitting in ancient times was the posture of authority. A child would be expected to stand in the presence of elders. Luke says Jesus was *sitting* – like a learned rabbi. Most teachers and preachers nowadays stand when they want to be heard. Not the rabbis; they always sat. Eighteen years later Jesus stood up to read Isaiah 61:1–2. 'Then he rolled up the scroll, gave it back to the attendant and *sat down*. The eyes of everyone in the synagogue were fastened on him' (Luke 4:20). Why? He was about to make a daring statement: 'Today this scripture is fulfilled in your hearing' (Luke 4:21). He made this statement after he sat down. When he delivered his most famous sermon – the Sermon on the Mount – he was in his rabbinical posture (Matt. 5:1). He taught one parable after another from the boat in which he 'sat' (Matt. 13:2). So his parents found their twelve-year-old son 'sitting among the teachers, listening to them and asking them questions' (Luke 2:46). It was a preview of things to come.

Therefore, in this practice round of what he would later be doing all the time, Jesus exercised his sovereign prerogative. Years later Jesus would turn his eyes heavenward and say, 'I praise you, Father, Lord of heaven and earth, because you have hidden these things from the wise and learned, and revealed them to little children. Yes, Father, for this was your good pleasure' (Matt. 11:25–6). For no one knows the Father except the Son 'and those to whom the Son *chooses* to reveal him' (Matt. 11:28). 'For just as the Father raises the dead and gives them life, even so the Son gives life to whom he is pleased to give it' (John 5:21). What was going on between Jesus and his parents – in Jesus being silent – was a taste of the ministry of the coming Sovereign Redeemer.

After the Feast was over, then, the best was about to begin. As far as Joseph and Mary were concerned, when the Feast was over – it was over. But as Yogi Berra used to say, 'It's not over till it's over.' For Jesus' parents the Feast was 'it'. For Jesus the Feast was but the occasion for his being where he was. And more was about to happen.

I don't know who said it first: 'When the meeting is over, the service begins,' meaning that when the meeting at church ends, Christian service in the world begins. But I think the reverse is sometimes true as well: when the church service is over the meeting begins. The word 'meeting' was special in ancient Israel. The Tent of Meeting got its name from Exodus 33:7: 'Now Moses used to take a tent and pitch it outside the camp some distance away, calling it the "tent of meeting". Anyone inquiring of the Lord would go to the tent of meeting outside the camp.' It was the place where God promised to meet with Moses, and God kept his word, for the Lord would speak to Moses 'face to face, as a man speaks with his friend' (Exod. 33:11). The Feast was over as far as Joseph and Mary were concerned but an extraordinary meeting was about to begin, with Jesus taking centre stage. Sometimes a church service will finish but God isn't finished. The meeting – with God – may suddenly take place even before people leave the building, and then remain for hours. That is how the Hebrides Revival (1948–9) is said to have begun. After a service was over, one man was found kneeling at a pew, praying aloud for Revival. He kept saying, 'Your honour is at stake, your honour is at stake.' God stepped in; within an hour hundreds spontaneously turned up at the church. Revival came to the islands and lasted for months. And yet any meeting with God often truly begins – whenever we go home – as we apply what we learned at the church service.

Some people go to church just for the service – the Feast, or ceremony – and some go to meet with God. Some go only for the ornateness of the worship, some truly worship by the Spirit of God. Some go for the preacher's oratory, some go to hear from God. When I was pastor of my little church in Lower Heyford (a Southern Baptist church near the old Upper Heyford air force base), Dr Lloyd-Jones used to come and preach for me. On one occasion an old friend of mine came to hear the Doctor preach. That evening the Doctor was at his best. All were enthralled with the power that flowed; God came down. But my dear friend didn't feel a thing. His only comment had to do with Dr Lloyd-Jones's masterful delivery: 'Not one split infinitive or dangling participle,' was the comment. That's all he got.

The real meeting was about to begin, but Joseph and Mary were miles down the road, believing Jesus was with them, not in Jerusalem. But the sphere of action was still in that ancient city. The Feast was but preparation for more to come. What made that particular Feast of the Passover historic was not just remembering what God had done in history but what God was doing then and there. What really mattered was the presence of Jesus in Jerusalem. It was as if the Tent of Meeting had returned momentarily.

Some twenty-one years later it would happen again. Had you walked into Jerusalem on Good Friday nearly two thousand years ago and asked, 'What is God doing in Jerusalem today?' the answer would be, 'Oh, don't you know? It's Passover. We are commemorating what God did in ancient Israel. The only problem is, there is a man dying on a cross just outside the city gate and we need to make sure he is dead so we can dispose of his body on this holy day.' No one – no one – would have believed at the time that the person dying on the cross was the real sphere of God's activity, namely that 'God was reconciling the world to himself in Christ, not counting men's sins against them' (2 Cor. 5:19). For the real fulfilment of Passover was literally taking place. Outside the camp, like the old Tent of Meeting (Exod. 33:7).

The Feast, the ceremony, the church service, the custom or tradition, then, is all some ever see. We nullify God's word by our traditions (Matt. 15:6). The Holy Spirit can be completely withdrawn and we wouldn't miss him, just like Joseph and Mary who hadn't noticed Jesus' absence.

Sometimes the hardest thing in the world to do is to *wait*. We want the church service to end as quickly as possible so we can get home – where our heart apparently is. Joseph and Mary wanted to get home. We do the same. On the other hand, if the Feast of the Passover was as ceremonial and ritualistic as many of our church services, one cannot blame Jesus' parents for wanting to start the long haul back to Nazareth. I fear that our services are so dull and uninteresting – with preaching being perhaps the main reason – that people are not motivated to attend church at all. Who can blame them for wanting it all to end as soon as possible?

As for dull preaching, I can never forget something Alex Buchanan said to me once:'We must communicate God as well as his word.' That shook me rigid. I always assumed that if I preached the word – God's word – that was enough. That, surely, was my calling. Wrong. If God *himself* is not experienced in the hearers I preach to, I have failed to do my job well. It is possible to preach the word without the Spirit. When Paul said that his gospel came not in word only – 'not simply with words, but also with power' (1 Thess. 1:5) – he meant that it is very possible indeed to preach with just words. I fear I have been as guilty as they come at this point. I pray those days are coming to an end as I make my way back to Jerusalem.

Some of us are determined to 'make' God speak, even when he is clearly saying nothing. We do it with the Scriptures. We make them say what they are not saying in order to fit them in with our own theological bias. I even heard recently of a church in the Middle East which has special information on fifteen years of Jesus' life between the ages of twelve and thirty.[4]

The old saying, 'Where the Scriptures speak, we speak; where the Scriptures are silent, we are silent,' is good sense. God doesn't answer the question regarding the origin of evil – why he made the world knowing man would sin and suffer. It is a mystery. Moses wanted to unravel the mystery as to how a bush could be on fire and that bush not burn up. So he said to himself,

'I will go over and see this strange sight – why the bush does not burn up.' When the LORD saw that he

had gone over to look, God called to him from
within the bush, 'Moses! Moses!' And Moses said,
'Here I am.' 'Do not come any closer,' God said.
'Take off your sandals, for the place where you are
standing is holy ground' (Exod. 3:4–5)

God's silence is holy ground. We must take off our shoes,
and worship.

But Joseph and Mary were not aware of God's silence.
They headed towards Galilee, thinking Jesus was with them.
Likewise, many of us are unaware of God's silence. We think
he is communicating when he isn't. We are on our way,
very happy and content, feeling we 'do not need a thing'
(Rev. 3:17).

We must therefore never be guilty of 'making' God speak.
Only a charlatan, a soothsayer or fortune-teller, *always* has a
word. Sometimes we do this sort of thing with the Bible –
opening it and taking the first verse we see as God's word
for the moment. God *can* do that – and I can honestly say
he has graciously done this with me. But if I am honest,
more often than not he tells me *nothing* by this precarious
method.

It's an old story. A distraught man decided he would open
the Bible as a last-ditch effort to hear from God. His eyes
fell upon the words, 'And Judas went out and hanged
himself.' This did not bless him, so he tried it again. His eyes
fell on the words, 'Go and do likewise.' By this time he was
nearly at the end of his tether but tried one more time. The
verse he got was, 'What thou doest, do quickly.' But that
wasn't God speaking at all.

God *was* with Joseph and Mary as they journeyed down
the road. But not the special presence of Jesus. God

sometimes lets us move on before the cloud lifts. We pay dearly for it. Jonah ran from the Lord and made his bed in the depths – but God was there (Jonah 1:3; 2:2; Ps. 139:8). He pleaded for God's *special* presence to return and God did (Jonah 2:4; 3:1).

When Joseph and Mary realised their mistake, they headed back to Jerusalem. We all have to do the equivalent of this: to go back to where we lost Jesus. But they didn't find him as easily as they imagined they would. I will say it again, it is always easier to lose God's special presence than it is to get it back. There is a way back. But only when we see how presumptuous we have been.

3

Finding out what pleases the Lord

And find out what pleases the Lord. (Eph. 5:10)

We learn what pleases those closest to us primarily by spending time with them. By trial and error we also discover things they like and dislike, and when we want such a relationship to develop it becomes fun to make the other happy. And yet this may not always be easy, even after we have known someone for years. For example, although my wife Louise has repeatedly said she doesn't like surprises, I never really believed it because I myself do like surprises. But I came to realise – after so many blunders – she really means it! Whether it be a birthday or anniversary celebration she wants to know in advance what plans I have in mind, and I now adjust to her wishes. She has also had to adjust to many of my eccentricities – like having no heavy discussions late in the evening or in the mornings before two cups of coffee!

The Lord has his own ways too, and he wants us to know them and adjust to them. We may think they are odd at first; but the benefits of accepting him as he is and adjusting to what pleases him will result in great blessing and peace.

That Paul would urge the Ephesians to 'find out' what pleases the Lord can only mean that this was an achievable goal – without the whole of the New Testament. Presumably they had only that one letter of Paul's to them (it was hundreds of years before all the Church had all of the New Testament as a source), which means they had to find out what pleases the Lord largely by experience – by trial and error. They had to spend time with the Lord and take seriously the warning not to grieve the Holy Spirit (Eph. 4:30).

We have the wonderful advantage over the early Church of having the whole Bible at our fingertips. This surely leaves us without excuse. And yet if we let the Bible replace the immediate witness, guidance and voice of the Spirit we quench him in one stroke. For we too must learn – by experience – what pleases the Lord. This means spending time with the Lord and developing a sensitivity to his ways.

Joseph and Mary knew Jesus better than anybody at the time. They no doubt felt special. After all, they were special. This, however, might give one a feeling of being a cut above everybody else. It happens to those who have experienced a degree of intimacy with God. If they are not careful, they will not only begin to take themselves too seriously but not tune into the ways of the Spirit which they may presume they already know so well.

I referred above to my own journey to get 'back to Jerusalem' and how upset I would sometimes get if I was disturbed during my quiet time. In my efforts to get close to God, so that I might not grieve the Spirit so quickly, I would get angry when called to the phone, or when my wife or children would interrupt me – and thus chase the Dove away then and there. My feeling was, 'Lord, here I am trying to get closer to you and you then allow these things to happen which you know upset me.' I thought God would provide some kind of indemnity on my behalf to show his approval of my spending more and more time alone with him. It became a vicious circle: I prayed more so I wouldn't grieve the Spirit and would grieve the Spirit in the process, and then I would be upset because I grieved the Spirit! It seemed like an impossible task at certain times.

This has happened in my time of sermon preparation as well. I need solitude and – above all – peace inside. My own efforts to prepare a sermon are invariably sabotaged if I am upset; all possibility of insight by the Spirit is removed. I would think: 'Lord, you have put me where I am. I have to have this sermon ready. What I will say publicly will be tape recorded and may be heard around the world. You've *got* to help me.' God seemed to reply, 'Really?'

I have learned that God will not accommodate me by altering the principles for me. He hems me in and requires me to adjust to the Dove. However justified I may feel at the time for being upset, hurt, resentful or angry, God 'stays behind' and lets me carry on – to my embarrassment. I have learned that I must sort things out if I am upset. The key is not God adjusting to me but my 'going back to Jerusalem'. It may require that I apologise – whether to my wife, children, deacons, members, other ministers or friends. It can be most humbling. But it is the only way I can function if it is the anointing I want.

Since God *could* overrule and commune with me as he did an angry Jonah (Jonah 4:4), why doesn't he do it? To be honest, he has. He has been so gracious. Otherwise I would never have survived. But he has tended to stop doing that, by and large (so it seems), and has taken my request for a greater anointing seriously. I have been constrained to seek his face all the more, apologise all the more (when necessary), forgive all the more and make the choice simply to be gracious.

There are therefore reasons God asks us to adjust to the gentle Holy Spirit. In this chapter I want to suggest some of them. Why won't God bend the rules for us? Why are we put on our own, as it were, to find out what pleases the Lord?

To mould our character to be more like Jesus

As we saw above, even the Son of God 'learned obedience from what he suffered' (Heb. 5:8). I do not know all that this means, but in my own experience, being left to myself – and not sensing God's conscious presence – is about the most painful thing I can think of. It is said of Hezekiah, 'God left him to test him and to know everything that was in his heart' (2 Chr. 32:31). As far as I can tell, God the Father never hid his face from Jesus except when his Son was on the cross and he cried out, 'My God, my God, why have you forsaken me?' (Matt. 27:46). My conclusion is, we in some sense enter into the sufferings of Jesus – that is, feeling forsaken – whenever God hides his face. If we don't, we should. For when I don't sense his presence, I want to know why. Having to adjust to the Dove forces me to be more like Jesus, painful though it is. I seem to learn no other way.

To produce greater obedience

Obedience is doing what one is told to do. We get our instructions from the Bible – God's revealed will. We cannot bypass the Bible and opt for a special 'word of knowledge' (often a 'quick-fix' solution) if we truly want to know God. The more we read the Bible the more we discover what God wants of us. God wants us to know him by knowing his word. Can you say you love God when you don't read his word and seek his face daily in it? The word of God doesn't adjust to us; we must adjust to it. When you are on a road with a map and get lost, the place you are heading for doesn't come to you; you have to look at the map again more carefully and adjust to it before you reach your destination. The Bible is like a map; it shows the way to go every day.

We are often angry with God at first for what he allows to happen – whether evil in the world generally or some misfortune he incredibly allows to happen in our own lives. But if we can learn to lower our voices we will eventually see that there *was* a good reason.

Let me give two examples. First, David's failed attempt to bring the Ark of the Covenant to Jerusalem. This was a noble and God-honouring idea. The thanks David got was that a man by the name of Uzzah was struck dead merely because he tried to steady the Ark with his hand when he thought it might topple over. It had been set on a cart pulled along by oxen and was to be brought for a mere distance of some twenty miles.

> When they came to the threshing floor of Nacon,
> Uzzah reached out and took hold of the ark of

God, because the oxen stumbled. The Lord's anger burned against Uzzah because of his irreverent act; therefore God struck him down and he died there beside the ark of God. (2 Sam. 6:6–7)

This made David angry. One can understand why. All David was trying to do was to restore the glory of God in Jerusalem! Would God be pleased? Certainly. But God wouldn't bend the rules for David, however lofty and honouring to God his idea was. David cooled off and sought the Lord. Upon closer reflection he discovered he hadn't obeyed God's plain word on the matter: 'We did not enquire of him how to do it in the prescribed way,' he admitted (1 Chr. 15:13). For only priests could carry the Ark. David had to make the adjustment to God's ways. He eventually moved the Ark to Jerusalem and all ended well (2 Sam. 6:14–19). The thing to remember: there *was* a reason things didn't work out at first.

Second, when Jesus stayed behind in the Judean desert rather than going to heal Lazarus as soon as the report came that Lazarus was ill. Jesus could have made it in time to heal Lazarus. But he waited – then showed up four days after the funeral! Mary and Martha each said, 'Lord, if you had been here, my brother would not have died' (John 11:21, 32).

In other words, it made no sense that Jesus didn't turn up. But at the end of the day it turned out that there was a good reason for it after all. For Jesus thought that raising Lazarus from the dead was a better idea than keeping him from dying. This simply shows how things that we don't understand at first can be understood later – if we will wait. This is true with everything that has ever happened that we didn't understand at the time.

To show how much we really do love God

We prove our love for God partly by our reaction to the knowledge that we grieved the Spirit. Our first reaction, like David's, may be anger. When we first discover that we have grieved the Spirit, it is often much like David not understanding how an apparently innocent thing like Uzzah touching the Ark could warrant such wrath from God. But, like David, we must mellow and think again. There is always a reason for the Dove fluttering away. Our love for God is shown by turning to him *again* and inquiring of him, as David did. 'One thing I ask of the LORD, this is what I seek: that I may dwell in the house of the LORD all the days of my life, to gaze upon the beauty of the LORD and to seek him in his temple' (Psalm 27:4).

It is a wonderful thing to realise that we really do love God, especially when we are so conscious of our unworthiness and inadequacies. But God lets us know that *he* knows we really do love him. I remember reading a book by the Puritan John Cotton in the Bodleian Library many years ago. He put it so beautifully, that there is no greater joy than seeing that our sanctification actually pleases the Lord. But what if God doesn't let us feel this way? In the absence of that assurance we must show we love God not by persistent resentment that grieves the Spirit so easily, but by persevering in seeking his face *all the more.*

So do not throw away your confidence; it will be richly rewarded. You need to persevere so that when you have done the will of God, you will receive what he has promised. For in just a very little while,

'He who is coming will come and will not delay.
But my righteous one will live by faith.
And if he shrinks back,
I will not be pleased with him.'
(Heb. 10:35–8)

However, as it is written:
'No eye has seen,
no ear has heard,
no mind has conceived
what God has prepared for those who love him.'
(1 Cor. 2:9).

To develop a sense of sin

There was a time in my life when this thought was alien to
me. That is, until I was baptised by the Holy Spirit. The
words of 1 John 1:8 then became real to me: 'If we claim to
be without sin, we deceive ourselves and the truth is not in
us.' Sadly, there was a time when I thought, 'I have no sin.'
But that was largely because of a faulty theology plus
excusing any sin as a mistake, error or 'shortcoming'. I dared
not use the word 'sin'. But that changed. Not that I began
sinning to prove I was a sinner, but because the greater
sense of *God* resulted in a greater sense of sin. It happened
to Isaiah when he saw the glory of God: ' "Woe to me!" I
cried. "I am ruined! For I am a man of unclean lips, and I
live among a people of unclean lips, and my eyes have seen
the King, the LORD Almighty" ' (Isa. 6:5).

When we discover what grieves the Holy Spirit we learn
more deeply what sin is. It has far more to do with what
we are like in ourselves than doing things some Christians

have called 'sin': kinds of entertainment, dress and what is commonly called 'worldliness' in some circles. Not that one always approves of such; it is only that not doing some things can give a self-righteous feeling and also masquerade as godliness. I've known of people who condemn the cinema and trendy dress, but who could have an out-and-out fight in the church's car park – and feel no conviction of sin for it at all! Adjusting to the Dove is to develop a sensitivity *to* him by coming to terms with what hurts his feelings. This is developing a true sense of sin. By this we further learn what grieves the Spirit, which leads to my next observation.

To let us see by experience the very things that grieve the Holy Spirit

Now they are all listed in Ephesians:

> And do not grieve the Holy Spirit of God, with
> whom you were sealed for the day of redemption.
> Get rid of all bitterness, rage and anger, brawling
> and slander, along with every form of malice. Be
> kind and compassionate to one another, forgiving
> each other, just as in Christ God forgave you. Be
> imitators of God, therefore, as dearly loved children
> and live a life of love, just as Christ loved us and
> gave himself up for us as a fragrant offering and
> sacrifice to God. But among you there must not be
> even a hint of sexual immorality, or of any kind of
> impurity, or of greed, because these are improper for
> God's holy people. Nor should there be obscenity,
> foolish talk or coarse joking, which are out of place,

but rather thanksgiving. For of this you can be sure:
No immoral, impure or greedy person – such a
man is an idolater – has any inheritance in the
kingdom of Christ and of God. Let no one deceive
you with empty words, for because of such things
God's wrath comes on those who are disobedient.
Therefore do not be partners with them.
(Eph. 4:30–5:7)

When we read these verses, they may tend to go past us like water falling off a duck's back. We certainly would agree that these warnings are valid. But it so often only flutters in the brain. My friend Robert Amess says that the longest journey for an Englishman is from 'the head to the heart'. But when 'the penny drops' and lodges in the heart our outlook changes.

Therefore there is a sense in which the very experience of noticing that the Dove has quietly flown away shows us for ourselves how real and true these verses in Ephesians 4:30–5:7 are! For there is a lot to be unpacked in these verses; discovering by trial and error shows the little things that chase the Dove away. That is, they seem small at first. Eventually they become very important and are incorporated into a lifestyle – because of a change in us – which would not grieve the Holy Spirit. After all, if the Dove *remained* on Jesus, our goal should be to keep the Dove on us for as long as possible and with minimal discontinuity of his ungrieved presence in us. In any case, one day God will take us all home where 'we shall be like him, for we shall see him as he is' (1 John 3:2). Learning how not to grieve the Spirit prepares us for that glorious moment.

To experience as soon as possible that the Spirit is grieved

As I have emphasised from the outset of this book, the Spirit tends to withdraw in such a manner that we feel nothing at all. But there is an exception to this and one of the chief aims of this book is precisely this: to feel it inside the moment he is grieved. If we develop such a sensitivity to his presence we will sense it the moment he is disturbed. Or if he is pleased.

When he is disturbed I begin to lose peace. It may happen when I am in conversation with someone. It may happen when I am answering a letter. An uneasiness inside emerges, a gentle signal that I am either saying something, listening to something or about to agree to something that is not pleasing to the Lord. When this occurs there is only one thing to do: stop. I may ask that we change the subject (in an unobtrusive manner), I simply may re-write what I just said. Following this 'check' from the Spirit (that's probably the best word for it) I spare myself of losing communion with the Lord, not to mention regret for other things down the road.

But there is a positive side: a positive peace that the Spirit approves. It is like a green light that sets me free to proceed in the manner I have been thinking. By this I know I am safe.

What is quite extraordinary (although we shouldn't be so surprised) is that following this 'check' (a negative feeling) comes a wonderful peace. As for the positive green light, it upholds that passage above (Eph. 4:30–5:7). It is as though those verses were a discovery of what one learned merely by obeying the inner testimony of the Spirit. That is the way Christians lived before they had the complete Bible; that is the way we today should live now that we have it!

To teach us graciousness

Paul said, 'Let your gentleness [AV – 'moderation'] be evident to all' (Phil. 4:5). This word comes from a Greek word which meant (in the ancient Hellenistic world) 'not to throw the book at someone but let them off the hook'. It comes down to our English word 'graciousness'.

Being gracious is a choice. We can choose to throw the book at someone – or to be gracious. It is a grace that doesn't come naturally or easily. But doing it is being like Jesus. It is the way God is to us; we show our gratitude to God for his graciousness by being gracious. Since I will say more about that below I will proceed with one more reason God will not bend the rules for us.

To show that we really do want a greater anointing

I am grateful to Dottie Oates, a friend of ours, who asked, 'Is it selfish to want to be filled more and more with the Holy Spirit?' She had asked that I pray for her in this manner. Then she began to feel guilty that this was her uttermost desire!

The truth is, the very desire for a greater anointing is supernatural. It is possible that a few years before, Dottie wouldn't have even thought of such a request! But as Jackie Pullinger once said to me, 'To the spiritual person the supernatural seems natural.' So it is not selfish, it is supernatural. But one can want a greater anointing *so much* that it seems selfish!

But there is more to it: we prove how much we want that greater anointing not necessarily by how much we go forward for prayer ministry at church or how much we pray in private. The proof of wanting a greater anointing is that *we grieve when we grieve the Spirit* and consequently adjust to him.

To put it another way: if you say you want a greater anointing more than anything in the world, I can safely promise you that you will get dozens of tests almost daily to prove that you really do mean that!

Adjusting to the Dove is not easy. It is inconvenient. It requires major changes in our habits that have never begun to bother us before. The question is, how far are you and I prepared to go in developing an acute sensitivity to the Holy Spirit's ways? I pray it will not be said of us, 'They have not known my ways,' as God said of ancient Israel, who forfeited their inheritance (Ps. 95:10).

Adjusting to the Dove is welcoming his presence but also giving him no cause to leave.

How do we welcome him? For one thing, tell him! Have you often addressed the Holy Spirit with these words, 'Holy Spirit, I welcome you'? Do this. Tell him he is most welcome. Doing this is, in my opinion, virtually the first thing we must utter to God, together with the prayer for the sprinkling of Christ's blood on us, every single morning of our lives. 'He already knows he is welcome,' you may say. Really? Do you not think he would love to hear you tell him this? When you call upon someone and that person says to you, 'You are most welcome here,' does it not make you feel good? Is the Holy Spirit so sensitive that he needs to be told he is welcome? Perhaps. Most people, sadly, want little or nothing to do with him. You can prove you are different. Welcome him! Intimacy is further developed by talking to the Lord about the most obvious and simple things – as you would do with a friend.

But welcome him to come in the manner he chooses. He may test your willingness in several ways. He may gently suggest that your attitude towards someone is not right. If you push this thought to one side, I'm sorry, but the chances are the Spirit may well unobtrusively slip away. You cannot be selective in the manner he may choose to come. When the Spirit departs like this, as I have been saying, you usually feel nothing at first. And yet you *do* feel something: righteous in yourself that your attitude is justified. You might even feel that God himself is saying, 'Well done. You are right to feel hurt.' But that is *not* the Holy Spirit. 'But I am convinced it is the Holy Spirit,' one may say.

I've been there a thousand times. I know what it is to feel so upset that 'they' could do this! I begin to have conversations with myself. I envisage what I will say to this person, what I will tell someone. I will put the record straight. I rehearse what they did. 'That can't be right,' I keep saying. I think I hear God saying, 'Of course that's not right.' I begin to feel good, that God is on my side – not theirs. I tell myself this is the presence of the Dove. Wrong. If anything, it's a pigeon. We will learn more of this in Chapter 8.

When I welcome the Holy Spirit I must take him as he wants to come. He may flood my soul with joy and peace. That is almost always my first preference. He may highlight a verse as I read the Bible, showing me something I hadn't seen before. That too is near the top of what I hope he will do. I love it when he applies the word to a current situation in such a manner that I *know* what to do that day. I don't like it, however, when that word points to having to apologise to my wife – or a deacon, friend or fellow minister – before I can feel great peace again.

We can be sure of one thing, in any case, however. The *end result* of the Holy Spirit's manifestation is considerable inner peace. Peace. It is wonderful and worth all the pain of having to move outside our comfort zone.

Adjusting to the Spirit, then, is welcoming his presence but also giving him no cause to leave. Before finishing this chapter I want to address the latter. What, then, are the things we may well have to do in order that we give no cause for the Dove flying quietly away? There are several things I want now to share. These things have come as a result of my 'finding out what pleases the Lord'. To the extent they might apply to you, I hope God will enable you to be blessed as you take them on board. What I now list mainly relates to those times when we are tempted to panic or get upset.

Letting things be. Don't try to straighten things out; let God do it – his way and in his time. This begins with an inward attitude – by deliberate and conscious choice. The assumption here is that 'things' that you were unexpectedly confronted with were negative and unpleasant. Speaking personally, my temperament is to roll up my sleeves, step in and 'fight fire with fire' – or criticise. Letting things be means *tongue control*. It ain't easy!

> Likewise the tongue is a small part of the body, but it makes great boasts. Consider what a great forest is set on fire by a small spark. The tongue also is a fire,

a world of evil among the parts of the body. It corrupts the whole person, sets the whole course of his life on fire, and is itself set on fire by hell. (Jas. 3:5–6)

The spark that can set a forest on fire is always present. What I say at this stage – and how I say it – can ensure that the Dove stays put. That is what I want. But the challenge can be terrific, sometimes (so it often seems at first) a temptation too great! But no. 'No temptation has seized you except what is common to man. And God is faithful; he will not let you be tempted beyond what you can bear. But when you are tempted, he will also provide a way out so that you can stand up under it' (1 Cor. 10:13). The 'way out' is, in this case, *letting things be.* After all, God has allowed this or that to happen. It may be bad news. It may be an unexpected confrontation of unreasonable behaviour. It may be a fierce accusation. It may be a severe disappointment. What am I to do? Nothing. Let it be. Leave it to our loving Heavenly Father, who permitted it.

It may be only a test to see whether I truly want the Dove to remain. In any case, it's the best way to live. To know that God is in control. 'You will keep in perfect peace him whose mind is steadfast, because he trusts in you' (Isa. 26:3). 'In quietness and trust is your strength' (Isa. 30:15). 'When words are many, sin is not absent, but he who holds his tongue is wise' (Prov. 10:19).

It is one thing to believe in the sovereignty of God in principle, quite another to believe it in practice. The proof of our confidence in God's sovereignty in the matter of practice is that I do nothing. No panic. I just leave it alone and say nothing.

Overlooking. This is unpacking the principle and practice of letting things be. It is the challenge of challenges when you are faced with an accusation (true or false), insult or any form of unfairness. It is therefore taking the principle and practice of letting things be a step further. 'A man's wisdom gives him patience; it is to his glory to overlook an offence' (Prov. 19:11). One definition of overlooking is 'to take no notice of, to allow an offence to go unpunished'.

This is graciousness. You act (sincerely) as though you didn't notice. I do not refer to social injustice in these pages, like 'refusing to be involved' when you see a crime; I am only referring to one's inner reaction to being verbally abused. Of course you defend yourself when you are physically attacked; you also step in (if possible) when you see it happening to another. This would not grieve the Spirit but, if anything, would be done by the Holy Spirit's power. I am referring rather to verbal self-control when you are personally maligned by a friend or enemy, a boss or a spouse.

'It is the glory of God to conceal a matter' (Prov. 25:2). This is what God has done for us by his Son's death on the cross. Our sins are concealed. 'As far as the east is from the west, so far has he removed our transgressions from us' (Ps. 103:12). For this reason we forgive 'just as in Christ God forgave you' (Eph. 4:32). It is what Jesus himself did (Luke 23:34). We conceal what could be told and brought out into the open. This way we ensure the Dove's presence. It explains how the Dove remained on Jesus right to the end.

Becoming vulnerable. This is not cowardice. This is not being a 'wimp'. It is in fact the opposite; it is being a tower of strength. It is what Paul means by becoming a man

69

(1 Cor. 13:11). It is when you are so strong inside that you do not take yourself so seriously. Vulnerability means the ability to be hurt, being unprotected. Our friend Alan Bell says that love is 'moving forward without protecting yourself'. Becoming vulnerable is therefore the opposite of the sin of self-protection.

Jesus was the strongest man that ever lived. He had the power to stop the entire crucifixion proceedings. He proved that by manifesting only a degree of his power when the chief priests and soldiers came to arrest him. Suddenly dozens (some scholars think it was hundreds) all 'fell to the ground' (John 18:6). But Jesus *chose* to be vulnerable. Paul said that Jesus was 'crucified in weakness' (2 Cor. 13:4), a chosen vulnerability.

Many marriages on the rocks could be healed overnight if both husband and wife would become vulnerable, stop protecting themselves and stop pointing the finger. I suppose tension in marriages is one of the chief causes for the Holy Spirit to be grieved today.

Taking myself too seriously grieves the Spirit and robs me of anointing. King Saul's taking himself too seriously led to his becoming yesterday's man (1 Sam. 13:9–14; 16:1). The issue of 'who gets the credit' paralyses many ministers today; we want to be sure we are noticed and given due recognition. When any of us is like that, you can be sure the Dove isn't even close.

This matter of wanting the credit always reminds me of the little plaque on former President Ronald Reagan's desk: 'There is no limit to how far a person can go as long as he doesn't care who gets the credit.' Many a person forfeits greater usefulness because he or she can't bear the thought of not getting a deserved credit for something. Neither can they tolerate someone else getting the credit for what they themselves did. I can understand this. But it is a wonderful inner release – glorifying to God – when we can be utterly self-effacing and abandon the praise of people. This way God can trust such a person with a wider ministry.

Setting people free. The ministry of emancipation is what Jesus and the Holy Spirit are all about. The problem is, we want to control. I doubt there is a much greater sin than deliberately leaving a person in the bondage of guilt when it lies within our power to emancipate them.

This means not only totally forgiving them by refusing to tell what we know, or keeping them from feeling intimidated and enabling them to forgive themselves, but also letting them save face. If you want to make a friend for ever, let him or her save face. This means to preserve their self-esteem, sense of dignity and assure them of self-worth. When Prime Minister Joseph of Egypt looked at eleven scared brothers and said, 'It was not you who sent me here, but God' (Gen. 45:8), he was letting each of them save face. They had tried to destroy him twenty-two years before and their guilt was unthinkably deep. Joseph knew that. He set them free. 'God intended it for good,' he said to them (Gen. 50:20). How that must have felt!

We can control people not only by guilt but by keeping them under our thumb in order that we can manipulate them. The Holy Spirit does not manipulate us – he sets us free. Many a strong leader (owing largely to insecurity) keeps their followers under control by making them feel disloyal if they do not dot every 'i' and cross every 't' as *they* would do. Such a leader, I believe, is in danger of quenching the Holy Spirit and robbing people of freedom. The Holy Spirit is in the business of emancipating, and when we enjoy his ungrieved and unquenched presence we will *keep* it by giving up personal control of people.

God does that to every one of us. He sets us free from our past. He promises that all things work together for *good* to those who love him, who are called according to his purpose (Rom. 8:28 AV). We have the high privilege of being Jesus to others – to set them free. The Holy Spirit loves this; the Dove is perfectly at home to those who behave in this manner. Letting people save face.

We may wish at first that God would bend the principles of the Holy Spirit for us. But at the end of the day we will thank God, who is no respecter of persons, for his patience with us and, most of all, for what we experience by adjusting to the Dove – namely, finding out for ourselves what pleases God.

4

Why is God sometimes silent?

Truly you are a God who hides himself, O God and Saviour of
Israel. (Isa. 45:15)

Oswald Chambers once asked a provoking question: 'Am I
close enough to God to feel secure when he is silent?' In
other words, must I have a constant two-way communication with God to feel approved and loved by him? One
of the reasons Paul exhorted Timothy to 'be instant in
season, out of season' (2 Tim. 4:2 AV) is because we must
develop a maturity that does not panic 'between the times',
to use Richard Bewes's helpful phrase. 'In season' is a time
of refreshing, when God clearly manifests himself; 'out of
season' is when he seems to hide his face from us. He is
silent.

God wants us to learn from his silence as much as he
does from his absence. For one thing, we perhaps learn
more about ourselves when God hides himself than in times
of conscious blessing. His silence is like sitting an examination in which we demonstrate how much we have learned
about his 'ways'.

Jesus silently stayed behind partly because of what he

himself was to learn and share with the teachers in the temple courts. But there was far more than that in the divine strategy; it was also for Joseph and Mary. It was probably the first 'practice round' for them as well. They had a lot to learn.

It is possible that they weren't prepared for the day they would have to relinquish Jesus for the purpose for which he had been sent to them. They could never forget the miraculous nature and circumstances of his birth. The angel Gabriel had been sent to Mary when she was a virgin:

> 'You will be with child and give birth to a son, and you are to give him the name Jesus. He will be great and will be called the Son of the Most High. The Lord God will give him the throne of his father David, and he will reign over the house of Jacob for ever; his kingdom will never end.' 'How will this be,' Mary asked the angel, 'since I am a virgin?' The angel answered, 'The Holy Spirit will come upon you, and the power of the Most High will overshadow you. So the holy one to be born will be called the Son of God.' (Luke 1:31–5)

Joseph also had been given a prophetic word in a dream:

> Joseph son of David, do not be afraid to take Mary home as your wife, because what is conceived in her is from the Holy Spirit. She will give birth to a son, and you are to give him the name Jesus, because he will save his people from their sins. (Matt. 1:20–1)

They may have remembered these events nearly every time they looked at Jesus. They therefore must have known that one day everything would change and they must let him go and release him to the Father who sent him. But surely that was a long way off, they may have thought. And it was indeed a good while before he finally left home for good.

But Jesus' bar mitzvah turned out to be a traumatic event for Joseph and Mary. It would be their first taste of what it would be like when he struck out on his own. And yet all he did was to stay behind in Jerusalem without explaining himself to them as they headed north for Nazareth.

Was it necessary that this memorable event take place, as if only for their sakes? Yes. Although Jesus was obedient to them once they headed for Nazareth (v. 51), I suspect from then on they felt a certain detachment regarding him that kept them from being too controlling. They had been put in their place even though they were closer to Jesus than anybody.

This needs to happen to all of us. Once we get a taste of intimacy with God we need a taste of his apparent aloofness as well. If that doesn't happen we almost always begin to take ourselves too seriously. We imagine ourselves to be closer to God than we really are and think we know more about him than we actually do.

An unusual experience with God is the best thing that can happen to us, but it can also be dangerous. We can think we are so special that the only thing which might save us is for God himself apparently to desert us. Spiritual pride is the most obnoxious kind of pride there is. To claim to have a unique 'hot line' to God is, first of all, *not* going to be something God ever gives us unconditionally. It would destroy us. It would make us smug, pompous and unteachable. People who suppose they have this sort of relationship with God are not only lacking in being teachable but probably also lacking in accountability. They sometimes think they are spiritually superior to all who try to help them. The only thing that will possibly help them is for God himself to 'do a job' on them. He 'stays behind' while they carry on in their presumption.

It happened to me, as I described above. It hurt very much and I couldn't understand it for a while. God appeared to betray me. He seemed to be like an enemy, as though he didn't know me. His manner of communicating and showing up just stopped. Not that I noticed it at first. The momentum and memory of a sustained intimacy over a good while masqueraded as his real presence. Until I came to terms with his absence.

It happens – I believe – to nearly every person who has had an authentic experience of the Holy Spirit. God hides his face – suddenly and without notice. No apology. Just silence. The explanation comes (usually) much, much later.

Why does God do this? Why does he 'stay behind'?

To show what is in our hearts

Moses warned the Israelites: 'Remember how the LORD your God led you all the way in the desert these forty years, to humble you and to test you in order to know what was in your heart, whether or not you would keep his commands' (Deut. 8:2). When we are on the receiving end of an unusual manifestation of God, we tend to feel so sure we will always be obedient. Peter thought it. 'Even if all fall away on account of you, I never will' (Matt. 26:33). He was so wrong. He thought he was better than all the rest.

Moses himself needed to experience the 'betrayal barrier' – a feeling that God has turned against you. Once Moses made the heroic decision to leave the palace of Pharaoh 'rather than to enjoy the pleasures of sin' (Heb. 11:25), he wasn't prepared for what immediately followed. Perhaps he thought that God would send a thousand angels to congratulate him. I only know he jumped the gun by anticipating an instant success and acceptance among his people, the Hebrews. He thought he had endeared himself to them by killing an Egyptian. Wrong. 'Moses thought that his own people would realise that God was using him to rescue them, but they did not' (Acts 7:25). He had to wait another forty years before he was ready to be used. As Dr Lloyd-Jones once said to me, 'The worst thing that can happen to a man is to succeed before he is ready.'

Hezekiah was one of Israel's greatest kings. He had seen God step into his life in an extraordinary manner again and again.

> Hezekiah trusted in the LORD, the God of Israel.
> There was no one like him among all the kings of
> Judah, either before him or after him. He held fast
> to the LORD and did not cease to follow him; he
> kept the commands the LORD had given Moses. And
> the LORD was with him; he was successful in
> whatever he undertook. (2 Kgs. 18:5–7a)

But that is not the whole story. His heart later became proud (2 Chr. 32:25). That is almost certainly why it is said that 'God left him to test him and to know everything that was in his heart' (2 Chr. 32:31). It is one thing for the manifestation of God's glory to do this by a powerful experience. As we saw earlier, God did that with Isaiah and he responded, 'Woe is me!' (Isa. 6:1–5). And yet it is another thing for God to make us see what we are like by seeming to desert us – staying behind. And we are shut up to see ourselves as we are. It is not a pretty sight. 'The heart is deceitful above all things and beyond cure. Who can understand it?' (Jer. 17:9).

To give us objectivity about ourselves

This is stating the previous point in a slightly different way. To have objectivity about ourselves is to rise above our feelings and prejudices. It is to see ourselves as we truly are, not where we have assumed we are. Or, as Robert Burns put it:

> O wad some power the giftie gie us
> To see oursels as ithers see us![5]

This means that God himself does us an enormous favour to give us a glimpse of ourselves as if through other people's eyes. It is a sobering experience. And if God does not do this for us by an immediate operation of the Spirit, he may use another to come alongside and tell us the truth. A true friend will do this. I have one or two friends who have the guts to talk to me like this. And sometimes the truth comes from our enemies. The latter may not have the best intentions, but if the truth of their words can be taken on board we are all the better for it. A true friend, however, is someone who knows all about you and *still* likes you – and will gently and lovingly slip in a word you need to hear.

The Lord 'stays behind', then, so that we will see what

we are like. It is true that his presence can result in an awareness of sin, like Isaiah's experience (Isa. 6:1–6). But it does not follow that his presence *always* does that. Indeed, it is his withdrawal from us instead that may have to do it. For it is so easy to take his presence for granted, as Joseph and Mary obviously did.

One of the most painful lessons I have learned was during my first year at Trevecca Nazarene College. I was eighteen and enrolled in a course called 'Introduction to the New Testament'. Towards the end of the term the professor said, 'Next week we get to the book of Revelation – which I don't understand, but I will try to introduce it. I don't suppose there is anybody here who understands this book, is there?' Yes, there was. Me. I raised my hand without the slightest blush on my countenance. 'Oh, Mr Kendall, do you understand the book of Revelation?' 'I do,' I said, with a straight face. And why shouldn't I? I had read a book on it. Moreover, my pastor Dr L.B. Hicks had his charts (in technicolour) that stretched a mile wide and several yards high. He lectured on Revelation every Wednesday night. I felt sorry for the deprived professor. Then he said to me, 'Would you like to teach the lesson next week, Mr Kendall?' My time had at last come. I knew I was sent to Trevecca for such a time as this! I accepted the offer.

The day came. I lectured on the book of Revelation. I told all I knew. It went on for fifty minutes. The bell rang, the students got up – they were amazingly able to do so – and filed out. I was surprised that they were not in awe and that they seemed just a little bit glad to leave. I had expected them all to queue up and fawn all over me, and with not a little reverence as well. No. They all left the room. However, there was one fellow student who came to me, and I thought to myself, 'It's about time.' He asked, 'Do you always hold your head to one side and talk with your jaw going back and forth?'

I was humiliated. The dear professor kindly stayed behind. He thanked me. 'But what do you think?' I asked. 'I've heard all that before,' he said. 'Who knows, you may be right.' I was put in my place. I still haven't fully recovered, neither would I boast today that I perfectly understand the book of Revelation! But there was a positive fall-out; I was given a measure of objectivity about myself. The Lord stayed behind as I carried on with pompous naïveté. It was the best thing that could have happened to me.

My painful experience in trying to show off at Trevecca is somewhat matched by a similar story concerning a famous preacher. As a young man he preached his first sermon in a country church in Tennessee. No one said a word. As the young preacher was driven home nobody in the car was saying a thing. But finally one of the men in the car – a farmer – broke the silence, knowing the young man hoped for a little bit of feed-back. 'Well, young man, I'll tell you. You went down the deepest and stayed down the longest and, I really do believe, brought up the least of anybody I've ever heard.' Now that was a bit cruel. But as my old friend the Reverend C.B. Fugett used to say to me, 'Every compliment, every bouquet, every pat on the back I ever received did perhaps a *little* more to make me a better person; but every jolt, every kick and every criticism always ended up doing me a world of good.'

For the Lord stays behind by letting the people we know be people, and the result, if we listen without being defensive, will bring us to greater objectivity about ourselves.

And yet it does not follow that coming to objectivity about ourselves is always by negative input. In 1970 my church in Fort Lauderdale allowed me to go on a course in California led by Dr Clyde Narramore. It was the first time I had sat in on a twenty-hour counselling session with a dozen others. The upshot of this for me was that I saw myself in a way I had not remotely considered. It was sobering, but it also encouraged me to see some positive aspects of my personality that gave me a measure of confidence.

To see what our reaction will be

Will we carry on, thinking God is with us, or will we notice his absence at once? Joseph and Mary did not miss his presence because they thought he *was* present. As far as we know, Jesus had never done anything like that before, so why should they think he was not there?

There possibly has to be a memorable first time! God hides his face. It may be abrupt – sudden, so that it is immediately noticeable. It may be sensed by an acute sense of loss. It may come by discovering you got it wrong on an opinion you held or by a bit of bad advice you gave another. You may have thought God gave you a definite word, only to discover later that it could not really have come from God after all.

I have referred above to those words about Hezekiah, 'God left him to test him and to know everything that was in his heart' (2 Chr. 32:31). God wanted to see what Hezekiah's reaction would be. For as long as the Lord is *consciously* with us, there usually isn't much of a test to our faith.

How tedious and tasteless the hours
When Jesus no longer I see;
Sweet prospects, sweet birds and sweet flowers
Have lost all their sweetness to me.
The midsummer sun shines but dim,
The fields strive in vain to look gay;
But when I am happy in Him
December's as pleasant as May.

(John Newton, 1725–1807)

There comes a time when, after being 'tutored' by the Lord, he steps back and sees how we do, as it were, on our own. My parents tell me that I began to walk when I was about ten months old. They taught me to walk by pinning a nappy around my waist. They held the nappy and walked beside me but eventually stayed behind as I walked on. When I saw that they weren't next to me, I fell down and cried. And yet I showed I could walk. The nappy around my waist made me feel I had them as well. Sometimes we all do that; we feel something that tells us Jesus is there when in fact we are tied to our comfort zone.

A well-known story comes out of Charles G. Finney's era. On one occasion he kept a great crowd waiting. Several hymns were sung, but no Finney. He was on the premises, those who were in charge of the meeting knew that. But when the time came for him to be introduced, he had not appeared. A man was sent back to the vestry and heard Finney's voice trembling behind the closed door: 'I won't go out there unless you go with me.' This was reported to what had been a restless congregation. But they now gladly waited. It was worth waiting for. When Finney finally appeared a great anointing settled on the congregation.

Without his uttering a word, scores of people rushed to the front and fell on their knees to pray and confess their sins. It is much like the time when Moses said, 'If your Presence does not go with us, do not send us up from here' (Exod. 33:15).

I have a sermon based on Hebrews 4:16 that I have preached countless times. Nearly every preacher has his 'sugar stick' and that one is probably mine. In January 1996 I was invited by John Arnott to preach at the Airport Christian Fellowship in Toronto on the second anniversary of the so-called Toronto Blessing.[6] I couldn't decide what to preach. The truth is, God gave me nothing. But when I was introduced I resorted to my sugar stick. I read Hebrews 4:14–16 with great difficulty. I had never had this problem before. But when I started to preach, I couldn't make sense of a single sentence. The congregation loved every minute of it. There was my wife Louise sitting right behind John and Carole Arnott uncontrollably laughing. Next to her was Lyndon Bowring, doing just the same. I tried to ignore them. For the second and third time I started: 'The Epistle to the Hebrews was written to discouraged Christians,' and the crowd was now really beginning to take off. They could see what was happening to me, and I was not enjoying it one bit. I was completely unable to proceed. It was like a nightmare, and yet I hoped it was. I was praying like mad. God seemed a million miles away to me.

'God help me,' I uttered with all my heart and strength. I tried a fourth time: 'This verse answers a lot of questions.' The crowd was now laughing with such volume that all I could think of was this word – or rather, lack of it – reaching across the Atlantic and giving ammunition to all my critics who felt I was abandoning my expository preaching ministry for the sake of the Toronto Blessing. I knew that if I failed to preach that night, and fell on the floor (my worst fear) in front of four thousand people and several video cameras, I would play right into the hands of all who were waiting to say, 'I told you so.' I tried a fifth time: 'A sentence that asks a question is called an interrogatory sentence.' The crowd by now could see God at work – seeing me trying helplessly to carry on. God at work? Yes.

I have never experienced anything like it in my life. Had someone offered me one million pounds in cash, tax-free, to preach this sermon I have preached over fifty times, I could not have done it. I have never been drunk unless it was on this occasion. But I tried again: 'This verse answers a lot of questions; who, how, what . . .' I couldn't say more. I called on all the brainpower and energy at my disposal. The Lord stayed behind, only in this case I could not preach that sermon at all. After fifteen minutes of this, mercifully, a word came into my head: Hebrews 13:13. I quickly turned to see what it said as the congregation reached a peak: 'Let us, then, go to him outside the camp, bearing the disgrace he bore.'

All of a sudden I had presence of mind. In seconds the laughter subsided. You could almost hear a pin drop. Without any notes or preparation I began preaching on the need to go outside the camp, bearing the reproach of Jesus. A half hour later, over two hundred, including many ministers, came forward when I gave an appeal. I continue to run into people who tell me their lives were changed that night. But why didn't God give me Hebrews 13:13 before I went up to the platform? You tell me. I only know now – I put it all together later – *that was the first day* the name of the church was changed from Airport Vineyard Fellowship to

Airport Christian Fellowship. That church had just been disenfranchised and were now outside the camp.

To see what we have learned in his presence once we are, as it were, 'on our own'

If we collapse the moment the Lord withdraws his special presence it suggests we haven't learned much. While we dare not proceed without him, sometimes we have no choice but to get on with our calling and make the most of the situation. I doubt that the Lord expects me to wait in the vestry like Charles Finney did every Sunday morning. I fear that if I did, I might never go out at all.

The late Bishop Festo Kivenge told of a row he and his wife had just before he was scheduled to preach. As he proceeded out of the door the Lord said, 'Don't go.' Festo argued with the Lord. 'But I must.' The Lord replied, 'Don't go.' Festo stuck to his guns. 'I have to go, the people are waiting.' Then the Lord said, 'You go on, but I will stay here with Mary.' Festo stayed and put things right with his wife before he proceeded.

I try to spend a certain amount of time every day in quiet before the Lord. In the perfect world I will feel his presence, read his word with full assurance of understanding and go out to do my job with great confidence. But it isn't always like that. In fact, it is not very often that I feel a great sense of God in my quiet time. The trouble with the old spiritual, 'Every time I feel the Spirit moving in my heart I'll pray', is that if I truly waited to feel the Spirit moving in my heart before I prayed I would pray very little. This is partly why Paul told us to 'be prepared in season and out of season' (2 Tim. 4:2). For 'in season' is when God's special presence is *felt*; 'out of season' is when he chooses to stay behind – to see if we will put into practice the things we learned in his presence. It takes greater faith and devotion to pray, trust and obey when God is absent than when he is present. I suspect we please God more by being faithful 'out of season' than by being faithful 'in season'. For more faith is required 'out of season'. 'And without faith it is impossible to please God, because anyone who comes to him must believe that he exists and that he rewards those who earnestly seek him' (Heb. 11:6).

There is a sense in which we can get emotionally tied to the Lord in an unhealthy manner. This is partly why Jesus stayed behind – not that he knew he was doing it for this particular reason. But he was under his Father's orders. Joseph and Mary needed to develop a healthy detachment from Jesus. I only know that Jesus did this later many times with his disciples. He sent out the Twelve (Matt. 10:5–15) and the seventy-two (Luke 10:1–12) without himself being personally at hand. They needed to be on their own, as it were, to put into practice what they had learned personally from Jesus. This is partly why he made the disciples get into a boat and 'go on ahead of him' (Matt. 14:22). This is probably why he did not stay with the Eleven the whole time after his resurrection; for forty days Jesus would come and go.

The special anointing of the Spirit is much the same. I am required to carry on whether or not I *feel* him present. If I didn't, I would never go out much at all, not to mention showing I had not learned much from his presence and his word.

Lest we take ourselves too seriously

The proof that Joseph and Mary took themselves too
seriously is that they reacted as they did once they found
Jesus in the temple courts several days later. 'Son, why
have you treated *us* like this?' (Luke 2:48). They not only
focused on themselves but were annoyed that Jesus had
kept silent and did not inform them he was staying behind
in Jerusalem.

This too is a problem I myself face nearly every day. One
of my greatest fears is that God will pass me by instead of
giving a greater anointing because I might take myself too
seriously. Taking ourselves too seriously is assuming we
are more important than we really are. It results in our
expecting more respect and attention than is warranted. It
is the feeling that we, if anyone, should be notified the
moment God has new plans for his Church – and that such
plans should include us.

Jesus demonstrated this point by his parable of the
workers in the vineyard. All had agreed on a stipulated sum
of money for their contract to work. But those who turned
up towards the end of the day received the same pay as
those who had worked all day. This caused a lot of mur-
muring. ' "These men who were hired last worked only
one hour," they said, "and you have made them equal to us
who have borne the burden of the work and the heat of
the day" ' (Matt. 20:12). For those who had worked the
longest, and possibly the hardest, expected to receive more.
But the landowner answered,

'Friend, I am not being unfair to you. Didn't you
agree to work for a denarius? Take your pay and go.

I want to give the man who was hired last the same as I gave you. Don't I have the right to do what I want with my own money? Or are you envious because I am generous?' So the last will be first, and the first will be last. (Matt. 20:13–16)

When we have worked long and hard we begin to presume that this will get the most recognition. But if others get this recognition and status who are Johnny-come-lately's, it gets our goat! And yet it only shows how self-righteous we are. When we get to Heaven I will not be surprised to learn that the disciples like Peter and John initially resented the abundant grace given to Saul of Tarsus. Instead of divine wrath and judgment coming down on Saul's head, he gets mercy and grace! The angels may have said to God, 'Aren't you going to punish this man Saul of Tarsus?' If so, God said, 'I just think I will change Saul and give him a ministry.' The truth is, the apostle Paul was given more insight and understanding than all the rest! I do not think it was easy for Peter and John to step aside for Paul.

God has a way of putting each of us in our place. But if we truly affirm him as a God of glory and sovereignty, we should be the last to be surprised when he chooses the unexpected vessel for his honour. When God said to Moses, 'I will have mercy on whom I will have mercy' (Exod. 33:19), we should not be upset when he demonstrates this sovereign right. At the end of the day not a single one of us has a right to take ourselves too seriously. After all, God has shown mercy to us already!

Even when we are seeking to walk in obedience to the Lord there is also a danger of taking ourselves too seriously. We may fall prey to the 'Elijah complex'. Elijah's finest hour was followed by his taking himself very seriously. 'I am the only one left,' he said, having earlier lamented he was no better than his ancestors. But God nonetheless manifested his glory in an unexpected manner: 'a gentle whisper' (1 Kgs. 19:4–12).

The twin sins of self-righteousness and self-pity so readily lift their ugly heads in us. For example, it is a rare person who can be an intercessor in prayer and not boast about it. It is a rare person who can pray for their leader and then refrain from giving advice. It is a rare person who can be greatly used of God today and be quietly willing to watch God use another tomorrow. It is a rare person who can see God answer prayer on one item and not question because he doesn't answer other prayers. It is a rare person who can enjoy sweet intimacy with Christ today and not feel sad when he doesn't manifest his presence tomorrow.

Few of us can handle much success, especially in the area of knowing God. God is the only one who can deal with us when we are like that. Sometimes the only way he can get our attention is by being ruthlessly silent.

5

The danger of presumption

Thinking he was in their company... (Luke 2:44)

In late 1994 several British Christian leaders met in a London hotel to pray about the Toronto Blessing. At the beginning of that year the Holy Spirit came down in an unusual manner at the Airport Vineyard Church in Toronto, now called Airport Christian Fellowship. This extraordinary phenomenon, characterised largely by people falling on the floor and laughing through the laying on of hands, made its way to London, notably at Holy Trinity Brompton. From there it spread like wildfire all over London and all over Britain. As a result about thirty leaders came together, meeting for nearly twenty-four hours in a London hotel for prayer and guidance. The group included leaders from various streams; some were in favour of the Toronto phenomenon, some against, some fairly neutral.

We began praying around four o'clock on a Monday afternoon. We also heard one or two papers read that gave a historical perspective. I myself gave a brief talk on 'What is Revival?' from Acts 2. During the time of prayer, which began with an open session and then turned into small groups, some of the leaders went from group to group with a statement they began preparing. This statement was to reflect on what God had told us as a result of praying together for the better part of twenty-four hours. But we had only *begun* praying! It wasn't seven o'clock – time for supper – and here came the beginning of a statement that reflected our time of prayer! I was a little surprised, but didn't say anything. I hoped others would see what was obvious to me, that some minds were made up before we began to pray. I wondered if the statement could have been written before the prayer meeting and issued without any prayer at all! Now, it did no harm and was drawn up with the best of intentions. And it was good that leaders of diverse backgrounds actually met to pray. But I ask, did God *really* speak? Did we *really* hear from God? What was the real point of meeting to pray to see what God was saying if our minds were already made up?

It is like a pastor in Kentucky who was struggling with his church when, out of the blue, he got a call to become the minister of a church in Hawaii. He said to his wife, 'You pack while I pray about it.' It is hard to seek the mind of the Lord when our own minds are really made up.

My background was characterised by a strict upbringing. I could not go to the cinema or circuses. Or to the public swimming pool. Although my old denomination was equivocal on the issue of 'mixed bathing', as it was called (boys and girls swimming together), my dad wouldn't allow me to go. But I kept begging to go. I was about fourteen years old. My dad felt I would be tempted to lust if I saw girls around me in their swimming suits. But he came up with a proposition: would I pray about it? Yes! So I did, and God told me it would be OK! Surprise, surprise.

It is to my dad's everlasting credit that he let me go – and that he showed trust in my seeking the Lord. But I do also recall that I felt God said it was OK as soon as I knelt to pray! I suspect also that God would have had a difficult time convincing me otherwise. My mind was already made up. That was not the last time I prayed about something about which I was already persuaded. It is very, very hard to hear from God when we are not truly open.

It is often unwarranted presumption that we already know God's will and are so sure of his special presence that gets us into difficulty. If we have known his special presence up to a certain point, we so easily assume that presence will stay with us, especially if we are in our comfort zone.

In this chapter we will focus on these words: 'Thinking he was in their company' (Luke 2:44). The Authorized Version says, 'Supposing him to have been in the company'. It is an easy mistake to make, especially when we are preoccupied with what seems right and true. Mary Magdalene was looking at Jesus with tear-filled eyes, '*thinking* he was the gardener' (John 20:15). The same Greek word is used again when Peter was miraculously delivered from prison: he '*thought* he was seeing a vision' (Acts 12:9). Jacob saw Joseph's coat stained with blood and presumed the worst. 'It is my son's robe! Some ferocious animal has devoured him. Joseph has surely been torn to pieces' (Gen. 37:33). He wasn't; he was very much alive.

Presumption. It is an easy thing to take on board. But in many cases it can be costly. It is so hard not to presume. It is a word that means 'to take for granted', or 'to suppose to be true'. I believe that we should pray every day to beware of presumption. It is assuming something to be true without the evidence. False assumptions have led many people into difficulty and some to destruction. One of the scariest of the proverbs is this: 'There is a way that seems right to a man, but in the end it leads to death' (Prov. 14:12).

What did Joseph and Mary presume? In a word: that Jesus moved with them just because they moved. That was reasonable to presume at the time. There was no reason to think otherwise. But it was a lesson they never forgot. It could have been the most traumatic moment for Mary, that is, between Jesus' birth and his public ministry. I only know that it was the only event of that era she apparently chose to share with Luke. She could have told hundreds of stories. But she gave only this one. It was admirable and vulnerable of her to reveal how she spoke to Jesus – 'Why have you treated us like this?'

The chief lesson here is that we should not presume upon God merely because we have had a close relationship with him. Nobody was closer to Jesus than his parents. That is about as close to the Lord as one could ever get! And if they made the mistake of presuming that Jesus moved because they moved, how much more should you and I be cautious in this area.

What is worse than what they did is to fancy that we are closer to God than we really are. I often wonder, why God does hide his face from us – suddenly and without notice, especially after a time of great intimacy with him. I think part of the reason is to keep us from being presumptuous.

Recalling Isaiah's words, 'Truly you are a God who hides himself, O God and Saviour of Israel' (Isa. 45:15), I have tried to figure out why Isaiah placed these words here and not somewhere else. They don't seem to fit. But maybe that is the point; at the unexpected time, for no apparent reason, God chooses to hide his face. That means that he disappears after being so real. His presence subsides with no apparent reason. It *could* mean we have grieved the Spirit. But it may also be because we need to be put in our place lest we get too familiar with God. It is possible to develop an 'over-familiarity' with God after he has been showing himself for a while, answering one prayer after another and giving us clear guidance. We begin to think we have a 'handle' on him. That is one of the reasons he suddenly 'withdraws the light of his countenance', as the Westminster Confession of Faith puts it. We must never forget:

> Do not be quick with your mouth,
> do not be hasty in your heart
> to utter anything before God.
> God is in heaven
> and you are on earth,
> so let your words be few.
>
> (Eccles. 5:2)

Joseph and Mary not only presumed that if they moved, Jesus moved with them, but that if he had anything import-ant to say it would be to them. The truth is, he had a lot to say. Joseph and Mary missed that entirely because they weren't where Jesus was. What he had to say caused the professionals of Jerusalem to marvel. This upset Joseph and Mary.

I know what it is to feel angry with the Lord for speaking where I haven't been. When I feel I have been close to him and he to me, I like to think he will tell *me* if he is going to move powerfully, wherever it is. If I proved my love for God by putting my reputation on the line by hard decisions, does this not qualify me for being notified if the Holy

Spirit is going to act powerfully somewhere? No.

We have seen that the Son of God opted to remain silent with his parents when he had a ministry to the teachers at the temple. Jesus did not say, 'Don't go back to Galilee without me.' He said nothing. This offended Joseph and Mary.

God may choose to say nothing to any of us. We must not sulk over his silence but bend the knee to his right to inform or withhold information. He is sovereign.

There were certain ingredients that played into their presumption. It has to do with familiarity. What they were used to. They knew their son well. They knew his ways. Or thought they did. This was the problem. They were not prepared for him to carry on in a manner they were not familiar with. And yet they knew definite facts about him no one else knew. They knew about his birth. He had no human father. This proved he was the Son of God, and they should have come to this obvious conclusion. When Jesus later asked, 'Didn't you know I had to be in my Father's house?' he implied that they should have known. But they apparently weren't ready for this sort of thing yet.

We never are. We all want to maintain the familiar relationship with the Lord we've had for so long. It too becomes our comfort zone. Yes, we may have paid a price for the relationship with God we finally came into. But we want it to stay *that way* from now on. We may well have moved out of our old comfort zone to get to where we are; but where we are becomes a *new* comfort zone!

Yesterday's stigma (offence) is today's comfort zone. For example, had you sided with Athanasius in the early fourth century you would have – at first – been on the losing side. Athanasius stood against Arius, who said that Jesus was 'like'

God but not the same as God. You may have heard the expression, 'It doesn't make one iota of difference.' That came out of the ancient Christological controversy when the issue was *homoiousion* versus *homoousion*, the Greek words that indicated whether the Word (*logos*) was 'like' God (*homoiousion*) or the 'same' as God (*homoousion*). The matter turned on the Greek letter *iota*, or 'i' – which you find in *homoiousion*. The Arians were winning the day for years. 'No!' thundered Athanasius, who unflinchingly held to his conviction that the Word was God, very God of very God. 'The world is against you,' they said to Athanasius. He flashed his black eyes and shouted, 'If the world is against Athanasius, then Athanasius is against the world.' He bore the stigma. And eventually won the day. But it is no stigma today; it is a comfort zone. Who doesn't believe that Jesus is God – unless you are a member of a cult or one who denies the infallibility of Scripture in any case?

This kind of scenario has been repeated thousands of times in church history. A pioneer bears the stigma; the settler upholds it but in relative comfort. He or she settles into a way of belief handed on a silver platter but originally born in tears and pain. The folly is to presume that it continues to be a stigma when it has become nothing more than a comfort zone.

The Pharisees presumed they were the vanguards of the ancient stigma because they loved the prophets who had been persecuted centuries before. They thought that if they had been alive in Isaiah's day they would have stood with him to the hilt. But when the One came along whom Isaiah prophesied about, the Pharisees hated him. Jesus applied this very principle:

> Woe to you, teachers of the law and Pharisees, you
> hypocrites! You build tombs for the prophets and
> decorate the graves of the righteous. And you say, 'If
> we had lived in the days of our forefathers, we
> would not have taken part with them in shedding
> the blood of the prophets.' So you testify against
> yourselves that you are the descendants of those
> who murdered the prophets. (Matt. 23:29–31)

Upholding the ancient prophets was in fact their comfort zone. But to them they were simply being faithful to the word. They *were* in a sense, of course, but we must never, never, never forget that those who rejected Jesus and wanted his death were the most fierce in contending for the presumed faith at the time. Which goes to show that we cannot expect truly to uphold the honour and glory of God when we are merely sound in our doctrine but hostile to the way God is *applying* his word today.

Arthur Blessitt is the man who has carried a large wooden cross around the world. He started a coffee house ministry in Hollywood's Sunset Strip in the 1960s. He built a wooden cross which he nailed to the wall inside to send a signal to people who came in. 'If I knew I was going to have to carry it around the world I wouldn't have made it so big,' he later said. But God told him to take the cross down and carry it on foot around the world. He is now in the *Guinness Book of Records* for the longest walk in human history. Countless thousands have come to Christ as a result. Heads of state have invited Arthur into their homes. He stayed in the house of Israel's Prime Minister Begin. He has received the Sinai Peace Medal for his historic walk from Jerusalem to Cairo. He has spent time with Israeli generals and also with Yasser Arafat. I invited him to spend a month at Westminster Chapel – May 1982. As I look back, it was the most pivotal (and best) decision I have made since coming here. He turned Westminster Chapel upside down. We were forced out of our comfort zone. It was hard. The result was the greatest internal crisis in Westminster Chapel's history. We survived. But it took at least four years. I then said to myself, 'No more controversies for me. I've paid my dues. I showed I would be obedient.' I intended to carry on in my new comfort zone. But God had other ideas – he believed I was safer *out* of my comfort zone.

Joseph and Mary wanted to maintain the relationship with Jesus they had become comfortable with. They had paid a price – a severe price. They were the scandal of Nazareth. Jesus was seen as the illegitimate son of Joseph and Mary who couldn't wait to get married (cf. John 6:42). They made a commitment not to tell what they knew, even though that may have cleared their names, and were seen as letting down God's holy standards. So they bore an immense stigma. But even this probably became a comfort zone for them in some sense, as they got used to it.

Since they went to Jerusalem every year for the Feast of the Passover, they were obviously familiar with the custom. It had become a habit. It was part of their culture. Religious and spiritual though it may have been, it was all thoroughly familiar to them. They weren't expecting anything out of the ordinary to take place.

That, I fear, is where some of us are in our churches today. We keep the 'feasts' – Christmas, Good Friday, Easter and perhaps other 'holy days' on the church calendar. But nobody really expects anything to happen on those occasions that would be out of the ordinary. A couple of years ago I spoke on the subject, 'What if Revival came at Christmas?' It didn't, but neither did anybody really expect it. It would have messed up everyone's plans had it come, including my own. I looked forward to opening presents, eating turkey, watching the Queen's speech and my favourite movies.

The truth is, none of us is prepared for God to step in, take over, shock us and show up in a manner we are not familiar with. When Arthur Blessitt first came to Westminster Chapel, a lot of people were understandably upset. Our comfort zone was, as I said, seriously threatened. But we had said we wanted Revival more than anything, and if this brings us closer to it, 'We must accept feeling uncomfortable,' I insisted. And when things went from bad to worse, one deacon actually asked, 'Do we *want* Revival, after all?' The implicit answer to his question was, 'No'. For, as Dale Gentry says, if we can avoid genuine Revival, we will. What Jesus did at the temple during the time of Passover – after Joseph and Mary had had enough and wanted to get back to Nazareth – was edging towards what true Revival always includes: people being astonished.

'When he was twelve years old, they went up to the Feast, according to the custom' (Luke 2:42). The Oxford Dictionary says that custom is 'a usual way of behaving or of doing something'. That is as good a definition as you will find for what we call comfort zone. That is the way we want church to be. Dr Jack Deere has a striking sermon entitled 'Why go to church?' When I knew he was going to preach on that at Westminster Chapel I was sobered a bit. I thought – yes, why *do* we go to church? He gave new, refreshing reasons I hadn't thought of. In a word: if that which is out of the ordinary happened, people would have different reasons for going. Some of course wouldn't go at all. But the world is crying out for what is not mere custom but out of the ordinary, as long as it is authentic – like Jesus amazing the teachers of his day. And those 'closest' to him being upset.

The Feast of the Passover was but a ceremony. It was an essential part of the ancient Law and occupied a special place in Israel's tradition. It was commanded lest people forget what God had done in *c.* 1300 BC in delivering the people from the bondage of Egypt. The Lord's Supper, which Jesus instituted as the ultimate fulfilment of the Passover (Matt. 26:17–29; cf. 1 Cor. 5:7), is given to us partly lest we too forget why he came and what he did for us. But as the Passover Feast was upstaged by an extra-ordinary appearance of the Son of God in *c.* 8 or 9 AD, we should hope this might occur when we partake of the Lord's Supper. The historic Cane Ridge Revival (1800), called America's 'Second Great Awakening', really began as a result of the minister's bold openness to the Holy Spirit when his church was observing the Lord's Supper.

We are at home with a ceremony. This is defined as a 'set of formal acts, especially those used on religious or public occasions'. Weddings. Funerals. Baptisms. The Eucharist. Ordination. Confirmation. A second definition of ceremony is 'formal politeness'. Not exactly the way Mary treated Jesus after he had demonstrated a measure of his glory. People who are normally very polite can be the most outrageous and indignant when what was supposed to be ceremonial is upstaged. It is like the way Michal, King David's wife, reacted when she saw David 'leaping and dancing before the LORD' (2 Sam. 6:16) when the Ark of the Covenant came to Jerusalem. 'How the king of Israel has distinguished himself today, disrobing in the sight of the slave girls of his servants as any vulgar fellow would!' (2 Sam. 6:20). But David discovered who his true friends were. An unexpected move of the Spirit has an interesting way of doing this.

There was one other factor that cohered with Joseph's and Mary's comfort zone: familiar company. 'Thinking he was in their company, they travelled on for a day' (Luke 2:44). There is no way of knowing how many made up this company. But almost certainly they had two things in common: an interest in Jewish feasts, and the fact that they were from the same area, possibly Nazareth. Company may mean companionship, a number of assembled guests or people with whom you spend time. Joseph and Mary presumed Jesus was in their company.

We all need each other. We need fellowship. But what makes fellowship *koinonia* is the presence of Christ. *Koinonia* is a Greek word for fellowship. 'But if we walk in the light, as he is in the light, we have fellowship with one another, and the blood of Jesus, his Son, purifies us from all sin' (1 John 1:7). *Koinonia* is translated 'communion' in the Authorized Version when Paul discussed the Lord's Supper. 'The cup of blessing which we bless, is it not the com- munion of the blood of Christ? The bread which we break, is it not the communion of the body of Christ?' (1 Cor. 10:16 AV). That is how the Lord's Supper came to be known as communion. And communion with Christ is exactly what it should be, but this is only possible when Christ is recognised at the Lord's Supper. It is a wonderful thing to know that Christ *is* present when we have the Lord's Supper. Whether he is recognised or manifests his glory in an unmistakable manner is another matter, but he is present nonetheless when we come together in his name. 'For where two or three come together in my name, there am I with them' (Matt. 18:20). Jesus himself promised to be with us when we convene to eat and drink at his Table (Matt. 26:29). But it is extremely important that we recognise him. Some of the Corinthians didn't and they paid a severe price as a consequence (1 Cor. 11:30).

Joseph and Mary thought – presumed – that Jesus was in their company. The company was their comfort zone. It was an area of familiarity. They saw the same people, faces, clothes, possessions. That was good enough. But Jesus wasn't there.

I have often been amazed at how company can be so quickly divided according to how people react to the special manifestation of God's glory. The special presence of God unites and divides.

> Do not suppose that I have come to bring peace to the earth. I did not come to bring peace, but a sword. For I have come to turn 'a man against his father, a daughter against her mother, a daughter-in-law against her mother-in-law – a man's enemies will be the members of his own household.'
> (Matt. 10:34–6)

The cross unites and divides. It even unites enemies. 'That day Herod and Pilate became friends – before this they had been enemies' (Luke 23:12). It is startling how the manifestation of God's glory brings people together who previously were not on speaking terms! I have seen it again and again. But the reverse is also true. People who love what God is up to discover friendship and fellowship with people they had not truly known. So it works both ways. For people who *reject* what God may be doing in a given time have a strange way of finding each other. They unite against God's manifestations. And likewise people who love it find each other.

But with Joseph and Mary presuming Christ to be with them, it turns out he wasn't. They trusted their comfort zone – the company – but he wasn't there. Which also goes to show how precarious it is to look to people you know and to take for granted that Christ is with them in an intimate sense. People you know and love may not have the intimacy with the Lord you may think they have. The discovery of how people *really* are (when it comes to a solid relationship with the Spirit of God) can be a most sobering enterprise. The warning for us all is, never presume that those you like or love have the same robust zeal for the things of God that you may have. You too may think, as Joseph and Mary did, that Christ is in your company of relatives and friends.

My guess is, for some of us, the Toronto Blessing became a comfort zone. In 1994 it possibly represented the most horrible stigma imaginable. Many who opposed it were vehement, some irately lost their heads as much as those laughing their heads off at Holy Trinity Brompton. But praying with people in the way that once led to laughter is as natural now as singing 'O come, all ye faithful' at Christmas. There is nothing particularly wrong in settling into yesterday's stigma. I comfortably uphold the doctrine of Athanasius. So we must not reject yesterday's stigma just because it seems a comfort zone today. But let us not delude ourselves that we are bearing the cross of Christ because we are still fighting yesterday's battles.

Like it or not, God often continues to 'remain behind', as it were, to see whether we will notice it. That is his style, always staying behind so that the new sphere of action will show if we are still wanting his glory. The big mistake we must avoid is to presume that God's special presence is with us just because we once enjoyed this, and presume we already know what he is up to.

6

How we can become insensitive to the Spirit

They seem eager to know my ways. (Isa. 58:2)

When I was a boy my dad always listened to a live radio broadcast (while he shaved and got ready for work) from the Cadle Tabernacle in Indianapolis, Indiana. Each morning at 6.15 came the opening song:

> Ere you left your room this morning
> Did you think to pray?

The theme of those lines was ingrained in me from my earliest days. My dad for one took this very seriously and always made a point of praying for thirty minutes every day before going to work. He was not a clergyman but a layman and had a prayer life which, I fear, puts most church leaders today to shame. The average church leader in Britain, according to a recent poll, spends only four minutes a day in quiet time!

According to Mark:

Very early in the morning, while it was still dark,
Jesus got up, left the house and went off to a solitary
place, where he prayed. (Mark 1:35)

According to Matthew, Jesus also prayed in the evenings:

After he had dismissed them, he went up on a
mountainside by himself to pray. When evening
came, he was there alone. (Matt. 14:23)

According to Luke, Jesus spent the night praying before he
made the choice of the Twelve:

One of those days Jesus went out to a mountainside
to pray, and spent the night praying to God. When
morning came, he called his disciples to him and
chose twelve of them, whom he also designated
apostles. (Luke 6:12–13)

If the Son of God needed to pray, how much more do we?
I find it extraordinary that Jesus prayed. After all, he was the
God-man. He kept his eyes constantly on the Father, never
making a move without the Father's beckoning (John 5:19,
30). It is a mystery to me that Jesus prayed at all, but he did,
possibly to ensure that he never moved ahead of the Father's
will.

When we become insensitive to the Spirit, chances are
we are unaware of it at first. Like being asleep: we don't
know we have been asleep until we wake up. In the meantime, we are filled with our own ways. It is a most precarious
position to be in. One way to avoid becoming insensitive
to the Spirit is by guarding our relationship with him when

we know we are hearing him, neither quenching nor grieving him.

I only know that Joseph and Mary would not have moved on without Jesus had they kept their eyes fastened on him all the time. If we keep our eyes on Jesus we can be spared much regret. I therefore ask: how can it also happen to us, how can we repeat their mistake?

By not earnestly seeking the mind of the Lord constantly

'In all your ways acknowledge him, and he will make your paths straight' (Prov. 3:6). This is a wonderful proverb and a wonderful promise. 'All your ways' must refer to anything that pertains to us. Some people worry that they should bother God with small things. But as Pastor Jim Cymbala puts it, 'Don't worry about bringing small things to God, for with God everything is small!' After all, Jesus said, 'Whoever can be trusted with very little can also be trusted with much, and whoever is dishonest with very little will also be dishonest with much' (Luke 16:10). It is much easier to bring the more difficult requests to God when we are in a daily habit of bringing *everything* to him already:

> O what peace we often forfeit,
> O what needless pain we bear,
> All because we do not carry
> Everything to God in prayer.
> (Joseph Medicott Scriven, 1819–86)

One of the sadder moments in the life of Joshua was the way in which he and Israel were lied to and deceived by the Gibeonites. Moses had warned them before he died, 'Make no treaty' with any of the inhabitants of Canaan (Deut. 7:1–2). But the Gibeonites ingeniously manipulated their way into Joshua's good graces and, before he realised what was happening, 'Then Joshua made a treaty of peace with them to let them live, and the leaders of the assembly ratified it by oath' (Josh. 9:15). Soon afterwards they realised they had been tricked. 'But all the leaders answered, "We have given them our *oath* by the LORD, the God of Israel, and we cannot touch them now" ' (Josh. 9:19). And yet all this happened because they, incredibly, 'did not inquire of the LORD' (Josh. 9:14). At their fingertips were the faithful means of knowing God's will, and they bypassed them.

We do the same thing when we do not talk to God about *everything*. Everything. If God let Joseph and Mary and Joshua move ahead without keeping their eyes diligently on the Lord, none of us should be surprised when we get into unnecessary difficulty. I myself have wound up even doing things like accepting invitations and engagements I should have declined – all because I said, 'Yes,' too rashly. Too often, when the time comes to fulfil them, I say, 'Whyever did I agree to do this?' I now pray more carefully over every little opportunity that comes my way.

I am gullible, especially when it comes to flattery. If someone compliments my preaching, for example, I fear I am too often like putty in their hands. My wife used to warn me about one person in particular who would rush up to me after a service and boost me to the high heavens. 'You'd better be careful about that man,' she kept saying. Before I knew it I accepted him for church membership – which turned out to be a tragic mistake. I have learned to listen, not only to the Lord but also to my wife!

Israel had the Gibeonites on their hands for years and years. I too know the pain of going by what appears to be true, 'thinking' Jesus is right there with me, and having to live painfully with what could have been avoided. I now pray daily about such things as invitations I accept and people I take into my confidence.

It does not follow that every single time I fail to know God's will clearly he lets me do something stupid. He has graciously overruled my haste thousands of times and bailed me out – or mercifully led me all along. But I have now lived long enough to take seriously the matter of seeking the Lord earnestly and constantly in the big things and the small things.

Neither does it follow that every single time I seek the Lord in big and small matters I always get it right. I am still often in a situation like that time I prayed about going to the swimming pool. It is hard to be neutral, or open, when something *seems* so right. Or when we eagerly want something.

By going by subjective feelings rather than God's objective word

Feelings can be so deceptive. They are the product of all our wishes, fears, prejudices and past experiences. We may develop a 'sixth sense' of what is right and wrong. And this can be very misleading. What is more scary, we can be *truly* led of the Holy Spirit one day and *think* we are the next. And be wrong.

Joseph and Mary were led of the Spirit to take Jesus to the Feast of the Passover. It was the Law. But they jumped ahead once the Passover was finished, *thinking* Jesus was with them.

Arthur Blessitt, more than anyone I have known, taught me to offer the Gospel to *everybody* indiscriminately. That was surely right, for Jesus tasted death for 'everyone' (Heb. 2:9). But I had not taken seriously enough that 'everyone' also means all *kinds* of people. After Arthur led us to speaking to people on the streets we noticed that the type of people who stopped and listened to us were not always merchant bankers or members of the House of Lords. Our greatest number of converts were the homeless, tramps and beggars.

My subjective feelings had not led me to embrace this perspective gladly. Westminster Chapel has been a fairly middle-class church for most of the last hundred years. That suited me fine. But I was wrong to hope to perpetuate this. Jesus unveiled the scroll of Isaiah 61 and claimed that this referred to himself, such being his own mandate:

> The Spirit of the Lord is on me, because he has
> anointed me to preach good news to the *poor*. He
> has sent me to proclaim freedom for the prisoners
> and recovery of sight for the blind, to release the
> *oppressed*, to proclaim the year of the Lord's favour.
> (Luke 4:18–19)

God's objective word has so much to say about the poor and oppressed that I am now ashamed how often I played the role of the priest and the Levite who, seeing a man in trouble, 'passed by on the other side' (Luke 10:31, 32). I began searching the Scriptures. 'Defend the cause of the weak and fatherless; maintain the rights of the poor and oppressed. Rescue the weak and needy; deliver them from the hand of the wicked' (Ps. 82:3–4). 'He who is kind to the poor lends to the LORD, and he will reward him for what he has done' (Prov. 19:17). 'But when you give a banquet, invite the poor, the crippled, the lame, the blind, and you will be blessed. Although they cannot repay you, you will be repaid at the resurrection of the righteous' (Luke 14:13–14). When John the Baptist had second thoughts about Jesus being 'the one who is to come', Jesus replied: 'Go back and report to John what you have seen and heard: The blind receive sight, the lame walk, those who have leprosy are cured, the deaf hear, the dead are raised, and the good news is preached to the poor' (Luke 7:22).

Had you asked me prior to May 1982 whether we were trying to reach the poor I would have honestly said, 'Yes, but I don't feel *led* to emphasise this aspect of evangelism.' My subjective feelings made me uncomfortable having to reach out to people like that. Not that they were driven away; it is just that I wasn't *gripped* to try to reach people like that. But I wasn't listening to the Holy Spirit. For the Holy Spirit has spoken objectively in his word – whether I liked it or felt drawn in that direction or not. 'If I were hungry I would not tell you' (Ps. 50:12). That partly means God doesn't come down by an irresistible vision to tell us what he is feeling. And yet if we seek him in his word he *does* tell us when he is hungry! That is part of the message of Matthew 25:31–46.

A lady came up to Arthur Blessitt and asked, 'Why is it that the Lord always seems to speak so clearly to you, but he never talks like that to me?' Arthur replied, 'Have you ever felt an impulse to talk to someone you didn't know about Jesus?' 'As a matter of fact I have,' she answered. Arthur looked at her and said, 'Start listening to that impulse and the voice of the Lord will become clearer and clearer.' The impulse of the Spirit, like the dove, is so gentle that we tend to underestimate it. But when it mirrors the objective word, it is safe to obey it. And the dividends are tremendous: ever-increasing ability to recognise the Holy Spirit's promptings.

I refer to the poor in this part of the book if only to show how easy it is to go by our feelings – and not God's objective word – and miss out on so much of God's heart. We may fancy that we are so spiritual – until our comfort zone is threatened.

I know what it is to give my subjective feelings priority over God's objective word – and feel good about it. I largely dismissed having to concentrate on the poor on the basis that *others* have a special calling in this area. And that is in one sense also true, of course; I have since had to face the fact that Westminster Chapel is not called to be a rescue mission mainly to beggars, and that I should not allow some people to take over, which they began doing, and abuse our central calling – preaching the Gospel. But I was not listening to the Holy Spirit by not making sufficient effort to reach every kind of person – whatever culture or background – with this Gospel.

Joseph and Mary walked towards Nazareth without Jesus and felt good about it – because they hadn't missed him yet. This is how we all manage to avoid any of the hard sayings of Jesus; we let our feelings govern us. We do it with doctrine, we do it with practical teachings of the Bible. Early in our marriage I avoided tithing – and felt good about it – believing it was more spiritual to pay my debts to man rather than to God. Two years later we were *deeper* in debt. Our financial situation reversed only in proportion to our tithing! There it was in the Bible – God's objective word (e.g. Mal. 3:10) – but my subjective feelings won out. And I was the loser until I bowed to Scripture.

The list is endless as to examples of how we prioritise our subjective feelings rather than being subservient to God's word. Our subjective feelings – another phrase for comfort zone – masquerade as God's voice. I once asked a Mormon preacher which he would believe – the Bible or the Book of Mormon – should he have to admit the two contradicted. He replied that he would have to go along with the Book of Mormon. I fear we do the same thing with our subjective feelings. Whether helping the hurting, paying our tithes, witnessing to strangers, refusing to listen to gossip, not pointing the finger or keeping a record of wrongs, not giving in to grumbling or whatever relates to what the Bible is clear on, we so often go along with what we feel. Or think. '*Thinking* he was in their company.' And feel fine.

By not being accountable

It is my opinion that a chief reason people get off the rails is because they remain accountable to no one and feel good about it. 'I am accountable to God alone,' some piously say. That sounds good. But it isn't good at all. This is one of the best reasons for being a member of a church and under the authority of its fellowship and leadership. One can opt for a subjective feeling – 'I don't feel led to get involved' – despite the objective warning: 'Let us not give up meeting together, as some are in the habit of doing, but let us encourage one another – and all the more as you see the

Day approaching' (Heb. 10:25). The truth is, we need each other.

Many church leaders – some high-profile Christians – imagine themselves exceptions to the rule. The consequence is, not a few get into all kinds of difficulty, sometimes falling into sexual sin. They feel they are above the spiritual judgment of those around them and put confidence in nobody. When you hear of Christians falling into sin, chances are they were not accountable to people around them or over them.

We all fancy that we are the exceptions to the rule. We all like to think that our particular temptation or trial is unique, and therefore God lets us off the hook as a special case. This is to believe the devil's lie. 'No temptation has seized you except what is common to man. And God is faithful; he will not let you be tempted beyond what you can bear. But when you are tempted, he will also provide a way out so that you can stand up under it' (1 Cor. 10:13). God simply does not bend the rules for his people, not even the 'best'. This is why the Bible does not gloss over its heroes. King Saul became yesterday's man because he thought he was not accountable to anybody. King David, the only person in Scripture called a man after God's 'own heart' (1 Sam. 13:14; Acts 13:22), thought he could get away with adultery, but was found out (2 Sam. 12:1–12). Are you accountable? Are you surrounded by people who know what you are up to and will help keep you on the straight and narrow? I would urge you to be accountable to trusted friends and leadership. 'But if you fail to do this, you will be sinning against the LORD; and you may be sure that your sin will find you out' (Num. 32:23).

As I write these lines I know people who are in serious

trouble because they have refused to be accountable. They will not listen to those who know them – and love them. They get defensive at the thought that they should have to listen. Some consequently reject their friends for a new set of friends who don't really know them. And when those new friends begin to ask questions, they too will probably be spurned.

When we reject suggestions or warnings, supposing that Jesus is in our company, we will be sorry – sooner or later.

Through bitterness

We saw above that this heads the list of ways we can grieve the Holy Spirit.

> And do not grieve the Holy Spirit of God, with
> whom you were sealed for the day of redemption.
> Get rid of all bitterness, rage and anger, brawling
> and slander, along with every form of malice. Be
> kind and compassionate to one another, forgiving
> each other, just as in Christ God forgave you.
> (Eph. 4:30–2)

Any sin – when being committed – seems somewhat justified at the time. We sweep the filth under the rug in order to carry on. But bitterness is possibly the greatest deceiver of all. Talk about something that seems right! Bitterness always has a cause: some grievance, or injustice. Whether it be from imperfect parents, abuse, being lied about, being cheated on or being let down by one you fully trusted, we all seem to have fairly strong reasons for feeling bitter and holding a grudge.

The truth is, we've all got a story to tell. I myself know what it is to feel bitter and feel good about it. And even think the Lord is in my company! As I often say, for some it may take years, for some months or weeks or days or minutes or seconds; but eventually such people have had to face the hard truth that, first, the Dove had quietly flown away, and second, the bitterness was not warranted after all. There may have been a cause, yes. When you are betrayed or lied about; when Christians hurt your own children; when you were being distanced by those who no longer need you – one could go on and on – you think at the time you are quite right to be angry. Mary was angry with Jesus! 'Son, why have you treated us like this?' (Luke 2:48). Jonah was angry with God for not vindicating his prophecy that Nineveh would be destroyed. 'But the LORD replied, "Have you any right to be angry?" ' (Jonah 4:4). The answer: no.

Like it or not, the Dove will not adjust to us. If we want the Dove to remain it means we must adjust to the Dove. This means *totally forgiving* those who hurt us. I suppose the Lord's Prayer has made liars out of more people than any document in human history when Jesus told us to pray, 'Forgive us our debts, as we also have forgiven our debtors' (Matt. 6:12). But does that make God responsible for what we say and do? No. We must adjust to the Dove and *mean it* when we pray, 'Forgive us our debts, *as we also have forgiven* our debtors.' That means, as Don Carson says, 'There is no forgiveness to the one who does not forgive.' When I pray to be forgiven I am asking God to let me off the hook. When I in turn say that I have forgiven those who owe me, I have let *them* off the hook. In other words, rather than ask God to throw the book at them I am asking him to let them off the hook as I pray he will do with me. When I pray that *sincerely*, the Dove sweetly returns.

All bitterness at the end of the day is ultimately directed towards God. We may say we are not bitter at God but, when we analyse it, we find ourselves thinking either why doesn't God deal with this horrible person, or why did God allow this person to do this? In a word: how could this happen to me? It is because God let it happen. He could have stopped it but didn't. We therefore blame him. As Mary did. And Jonah.

Corrie ten Boom tells the moving story of how, in one of her services, she saw the very prison officer who had been so cruel to her beloved sister when she and her sister were imprisoned by the Nazis. Suddenly she had to rise and speak before the congregation. She cried out in her heart to God to be filled with the love of Jesus. God did it, she spoke as planned and met the man after the service. She found herself amazingly able to be gracious. The Dove remained.

Rodney Howard-Browne reckons that most people lose their healing and blessing of joy (that sometimes comes from the laying on of hands) mainly because they cannot totally forgive, and get bitter. They wonder what happened. The ailment returns. The joy subsides.

Many a bitter minister manages to preach with apparent effectiveness because he either knows his sermon so well or has learned how to 'appear' anointed, or simply because the gifts and calling of God are irrevocable (Rom. 11:29). That way God uses them. But it is only a matter of time before such people will see that the Dove flew away long ago and they will have to come to terms with the loss of the genuine anointing of the Holy Spirit. It is true with *all* Christians. We can play games only for so long.

In a word: when we keep a record of wrongs (cf. 1 Cor. 13:5) and point the finger (cf. Isa. 58:9) the Holy Spirit is grieved. We may not feel a thing – at first.

By doing what is 'righteous' but not what God really wants

When Joseph and Mary took Jesus to Jerusalem it was a righteous thing to do. So far, so good. But leaving him behind was not right. They may have felt very good inside for having kept the requirements of the Law by observing Passover in Jerusalem.

Isaiah addressed a similar malady.

Shout it aloud, do not hold back.
    Raise your voice like a trumpet.
Declare to my people their rebellion
    and to the house of Jacob their sins.
For day after day they seek me out;
    they seem eager to know my ways,
as if they were a nation that does what is right
    and has not forsaken the commands of its God.
They ask me for just decisions
    and seem eager for God to come near them.
'Why have we fasted,' they say,
    'and you have not seen it?
Why have we humbled ourselves,
    and you have not noticed?'

Yet on the day of your fasting, you do as you please
    and exploit all your workers.
Your fasting ends in quarrelling and strife,

and in striking each other with wicked fists.
You cannot fast as you do today
    and expect your voice to be heard on high.
Is this the kind of fast I have chosen,
    only a day for a man to humble himself?
Is it only for bowing one's head like a reed
    and for lying on sackcloth and ashes?
Is that what you call a fast,
    a day acceptable to the LORD? (Isa. 58:1–5)

The Israelites thought God was in their company because they were doing righteous deeds – like fasting. And yet, to their credit, they admitted that God took no notice of it. ' "Why have we fasted," they say, "and you have not seen it? Why have we humbled ourselves, and you have not noticed?" ' (Isa. 58:3). The problem was, they enjoyed their fasting and humbling themselves. It was like a game. Isaiah said that the Israelites of his day 'seem eager for God to come near them' (Isa. 58:2). So many of us are like that. We seem eager for God to come down in power.

It is easy to get so busy in doing 'righteous' things, such as being active in church matters, and think that God must be thrilled. He may be nowhere near but we carry on.

I think it is possible for God to be with us in one area and absent in another – at the same time. For example, in my effort to make my way back to Jerusalem early on in my ministry at Westminster Chapel, God dealt with me powerfully in certain ways. He initially dealt with me in two significant areas: complaining and bitterness. The result was a fresh renewal of the Spirit in my personal life and public ministry. I became easier to live with at home and my preaching improved some.

But there is another area of my life where I was, I fear, a failure. It has to do with my role as a father. I was doing 'righteous deeds' – preaching, praying and, yes, fasting once in a while. Books emerged from the press. Some people claimed to be blessed by my preaching generally and even my writing. But I overlooked my family. I thought – 'supposed' – that by putting my church and my ministry first I was putting God first.

The paradox is this: God was with me in one area of my life but 'stayed behind' in another while I moved on. There seemed to be a measure of anointing on my preaching, but I took our children for granted. I have paid a severe price as a result. I now think that had I put my family first, I would have preached just as well (probably better). But it is only in recent years that I have come to terms with this. I can't get those years back and all I now know to do is trust God to restore the years which the locusts have eaten (Joel 2:25).

This is why I believe it is possible to experience the real presence of Christ and his absence at the same time. Strange as it may seem, God can show his face and hide his face at the same time. He can be with me powerfully in one aspect of my life and allow the Dove to flutter away in another.

You may ask, why didn't God *tell* me to spend time with my family? He did. I didn't listen. I carried on. And yet he has proved to be with me in my ministry generally. It is not that God was not with Joseph and Mary as they moved ahead without Jesus. God loved them to the hilt – and brought them back to Jesus. But it goes to show how we can presume that God is with us equally and categorically in every single area of our lives – and be mistaken. We must not presume God is totally approving of all that we are and do merely because he is gracious to us in a particular area.

What God really wants is not our doing certain righteous deeds – which we enjoy – and neglecting what should have had priority.

> Is not *this* the kind of fasting I have chosen:
> to loose the chains of injustice
>   and untie the cords of the yoke,
> to set the oppressed free
>   and break every yoke?
> Is it not to share your food with the hungry
>   and to provide the poor wanderer with shelter –
> when you see the naked, to clothe him,
>   and not to turn away from your own flesh and
>   blood? (Isa. 58:6–7)

This shows that we must tune in to God's heartbeat. This will almost always mean doing that which requires more effort, and what may be (sadly) less fun, in order to carry out his *whole* will.

By forgetting to thank the Lord

Joseph and Mary should have been the most grateful people on the face of the earth. What an honour – a privilege that could never be extended to anyone else – to be the parents of the one and only Son of God! And I am sure they were aware of this and must have been in perpetual awe to be chosen for this service to God. But the fact that they could leave their child behind in the ancient capital of Israel shows that they in some sense took for granted his presence with them.

It is this sort of assumption that I suppose we all fall into. We take for granted the matter of showing gratitude to God. When we are truly grateful we will never let him out of our sight or move one inch without his conscious presence as far as lies within us. The problem is, we say, 'The Lord knows I'm thankful.' Really? Then we should tell him and show it.

In my own journey back to Jerusalem I have been convicted of the need to be thankful in an ever-increasing manner. My first awareness of ingratitude really hit home when I was preaching through Philippians, and came to 4:6:

Do not be anxious about anything, but in everything, by prayer and petition, with thanksgiving, present your requests to God.

The words 'with thanksgiving' sobered me. I hadn't really done this. I have prayed tens of thousands of prayers and petitions to God without thanking him. I will never forget something the great Dr Lloyd-Jones once said to me in response to my comment, 'But God already knows how I feel'; the Doctor said, 'Tell him!' Simple as that. Tell him.

I began doing that. I keep a journal. I record every eventful thing of every day of my life. I can tell you where I was at three o'clock on April 8th 1983. But after preaching on Philippians 4:6 (which, as it happens, was on November 13th 1988), I began a new thing and have kept it up literally every day since. I re-read my journal of yesterday each morning, to remind me of what I did, and I thank God for *every single thing I can think of* that I'm thankful for. It doesn't take long; less than a minute. But I do it.

Jesus healed ten lepers in one go. One – only one – came back to say thank you. 'Jesus asked, "Were not all ten cleansed? Where are the other nine?" ' (Luke 17:17). That's a pretty strong hint how much God cares and *notices* whether or not we bother to thank him.

Thanksgiving and praise lead to authentic worship, when we are carried beyond ourselves and sense God himself. It is a marvellous feeling. It begins with taking the time to say thank you to God. This is another area of my own life in which I had not taken the trouble to adjust to the Dove. I have sought to make up for this.

By not recognising the 'bruised reed'

If I were to recount how often I have failed at this point, I fear that the number of times would almost overwhelm me with embarrassment. And yet there was a time in my life when I would not have even thought about this. But one day something happened that caused me to see how insensitive I was to sensitive feelings around me. For one who has been at home in the fast lane, who seldom suffered fools gladly and who would think 'that should not bother this person', it was no small breakthrough that I was forced to notice a bruised reed before my eyes. It changed my life. This is how I was made to recall those words that describe Jesus, 'A bruised reed he will not break' (Matt. 12:20). This means that God will not hurt the person already hurting.

I do not like to think of how many times I have caused the Dove to fly away by my not being sensitive to the bruised reed. The bruised reed is a person who has been severely damaged. It may be the result of a long-term or relatively short-term situation when a person was let down, deeply offended, deprived of love, misunderstood, neglected, criticised or abused (whether verbally or physically). The result is a person who is crying out for love. They are desperate just to be accepted – for once. So afraid of not being accepted, this person often manifests behaviour that puts us all off – but that is their way of showing how bruised they are. Perhaps they are hypersensitive and not pleasant to be around, but the truth is, we're talking about a bruised reed. The list is endless. There are bruised reeds all around us. The chances are, you can find one when you look in the mirror.

We can become insensitive to the Spirit by not recognising the bruised reed that God puts in our path. The truth is, we are all bruised reeds and those around us are bruised reeds. When we begin to treat people this way, we will begin to be just a little bit more like Jesus.

It is a mercy from God when we sense we have indeed become insensitive to the Spirit. For in that moment we are beginning – at last – to become sensitive to him. If we come to terms with the way we tend to become insensitive to the Spirit, it shows we have not yet become so insensitive that we cannot hear him.

7

Recognising God's absence

Then they began looking for him. (Luke 2:44)

It might seem extraordinary that Jesus' parents travelled on for a day without recognising he was not with them. But their company included relations and friends, and they assumed that Jesus was part of the group. Whether they walked or went by a caravan of camels, we don't know. What we do know is that returning home was as routine as going regularly to Jerusalem for the Feasts. Routine of habit, if anything, made it rather easy to carry on without Jesus. They were familiar with the territory, which also made it easy to move on without him.

Routine of habit, even if it's a good habit, often becomes a comfort zone. There is nothing wrong with a comfort zone. We all have them. But perhaps we need to be reminded that there is an inherent danger here: the familiarity with the way we've always done things can masquerade as the special presence of God.

Take daily devotions, or quiet time, for example. Nothing is more important or special than that. Moreover, it is a righteous thing to do. And yet, because we are all innately self-righteous by nature, it can make us defensive and closed. I have known situations in which one bristles at a word from God, especially if it comes from outside our comfort zone, because we say to ourselves: 'As close as I am to God – because I regularly spend time with him – I would immediately recognise this manifestation as authentic if it really were from God.' For I have known some of God's 'best' people to reject what God is saying because they assume their walk with God is so in order it would surely be impossible for them not to know it when God is speaking.

Our private quiet time with God can therefore serve as a defence mechanism to keep us from hearing an uncomfortable word from the Lord. This is because we tend to do all the talking when we wait before the Lord. Our talking all the time may unwittingly serve to get us running ahead of the Lord – when he chooses to be silent or absent.

It is an easy thing to do. I know that my own slowness to accept what was at first most uncomfortable could be explained partly by my own smugness. You could not have told me I was smug and made me believe it. Smugness is a feeling of self-satisfaction. It is an attitude very hard to penetrate. This is why we should plead with the Lord to help us to be more and more sensitive to the Spirit. He may back away from us unobtrusively and let us move on, if only to see how long we will go before we recognise his absence.

The issue that emerges from this part of the story is, how long does it take before we recognise the absence of the presence of God? Luke tells us that 'they travelled on for a day'. Then they realised something was wrong. Luke does not focus on the moment at which they were consciously aware of Jesus' absence. Perhaps they were ready to settle in for the night, or getting ready for the evening meal. Whatever – it must have been a sobering moment.

Routine of habit is generally a good thing. We need the discipline to get up each day at a certain time to get out to work. We need discipline to take time to read the Bible and pray. We know how long it takes to get to work, so we leave home accordingly. Routine of habit when it comes to church is also necessary in many ways. We need to know what time the service begins. We accept that most services have a familiar start and style of worship and liturgy of some kind.

But God could be absent and not be missed because we are so familiar with the territory and routine. Even in the most non-liturgical service there is a predictable pattern. I have often attended a little church in Bimini, Bahamas, for years. They would probably claim to be, if anything, anti-liturgical, at least compared to the Episcopal and Catholic churches on the island. But their pattern is as set as any I know. The minister always begins, 'Say, praise the Lord! Say, thank you, Jesus.' This is their comfort zone. God could be absent and not be missed.

Jacob had the opposite problem. One evening he came to a certain place to which he eventually gave the name Bethel. He apparently thought at first: 'There's nothing here for me.' But he later said, 'Surely the LORD *is* in this place, and I was *not* aware of it' (Gen. 28:16). For God met with him unexpectedly and his life was never quite the same again.

It seems therefore that two possibilities – opposite patterns – may take us unawares: God being present and us not knowing it, and God being absent and us not knowing it. We may reasonably ask the question, how long does it take to recognise God's presence and how long does it take to realise he is not present? Either question may in a sense indicate a 'spiritual intelligence', or discernment.

One of the gifts of the Spirit is called 'the ability to distinguish between spirits' (1 Cor. 12:10). It seems that some people assume that this means only the ability to recognise the demonic. This is a lop-sided emphasis. For it also, if not primarily, means the ability to recognise the genuine Holy Spirit. It is one thing to be an 'expert' in the area of the demonic, quite another to be able to discern the genuine presence of God. If anything, it takes a higher level of spirituality to recognise the *real* than it does to detect the counterfeit. But sadly there are people who mainly think in terms of recognising the devil and seeing a demon behind every bush! It is just as important to discern when God is present as when Satan is active.

We cannot really discern God's absence until we have experienced his presence. Could it be that some Christians have not really experienced the special presence of God and would therefore not have a clue what is meant by his absence? I don't mean to be unfair, but I suspect either would feel the same to some of us.

The manifestation of God's presence can be unveiled in more than one way. Jacob felt the presence of God at Bethel and he was *afraid* (Gen. 28:17). That feeling of awe was what people experienced as a result of a healing presence in Galilee (Luke 5:17, 26). They felt this immediately after Pentecost (Acts 2:43) and following Ananias and Sapphira being struck dead by the Spirit (Acts 5:11). And yet in Ezra's day when the builders laid the foundations of the temple of the Lord many 'shouted for joy' (Ezra 3:12). And when Ezra gave an exposition of the Law, 'Nehemiah said, "Go and enjoy choice food and sweet drinks, and send some to those who have nothing prepared. This day is sacred to our LORD. Do not grieve, for the joy of the LORD is your strength" ' (Neh. 8:10). David said, 'You will fill me with joy in your presence' (Ps. 16:11). The angel of the Lord said to the shepherds, 'I bring you good news of great joy' (Luke 2:10). As a result of Philip preaching in Samaria, 'So there was great joy in that city' (Acts 8:8).

We must try to remain open to the manner in which God chooses to manifest his glory. For some there is a bias in the direction of the fear of God. That to them proves that God is present. Some would even be uneasy with joy. *Fear* is their comfort zone. They also have a ready-made theological rationale for not smiling and looking sad. When we don't have much joy we can hide behind the convenient view that God's glory always produces a sense of fear. And yet for some there is a bias in the direction of joy and happy worship. I recall a man at my old college in Nashville who stood up – right after singing 'When I survey the wondrous cross' – and shouted, 'Let's stop singing these dead songs and get some life in this place.' How sad, but that is exactly what he said. We don't seem to realise sometimes that a comfort zone so easily masquerades as what we deem to be the presence of God.

It is, at the end of the day, impossible to describe adequately the feeling of God's special presence – however it is manifested. As Ena Dickinson, a member of our congregation, put it, 'It is impossible to describe a good prayer meeting.' You have to *be* there. So with God's special presence. The Bible uses words like fear, joy, awe, shouting, praise, etc. But when we are on the outside looking in, as it were, we won't have a clue what this is like.

I attended a service at Jackie Pullinger's church in Hong Kong. Some of it was in Chinese, some in English. All I know is, I could not stop weeping. Why? I don't really know. I just cried and cried. The first time I attended a service conducted by Rodney Howard-Browne I felt a sense of awe. People were laughing – hundreds and hundreds – all over the auditorium. Rodney wasn't even preaching, only leading worship. While I was almost carried away someone interrupted my sense of worship and asked for me to be interviewed for something or other. The one who did this hadn't been in the service, so I am not judging him. I only know I refused to leave. I was enthralled with the sheer presence of God. It happened again in one of Rodney's services in New Orleans. I wept and wept as people all over the auditorium laughed and cried. I would have given almost anything if my own church members could have been transported to that service. I knew I could never truly describe it.

The special presence of God. It is greater than anything that can be said about it. You cannot miss it, however, unless you've experienced it. And yet it is possible, in any place where this sense of God's presence is *constantly* experienced, to suppose it continues even though it leaves. The momentum from yesterday, the memory of how real it was and the continued expectancy that it will be present today – all these can make one think God is present when he isn't. It is an easy mistake to make.

We may want to believe God is there. Our expectancy can go a long way, but eventually we have to come to terms with the fact, if it be so, that the Lord just isn't showing up as he did before.

All Revivals come to an end. All special manifestations of God's glory and presence come to an end. It does not follow that we have done anything wrong. Peter was excited that the Lord Jesus manifested his glory on the Mount of Transfiguration. 'It is good for us to be here,' he said (Matt. 17:4). But they had to come down from the mountain and move into the next phase of God's strategy and purpose (Matt. 17:9).

The folly therefore is to think God's special presence continues to be manifested when it isn't. Some keep it going – or think that is what they are doing. The Cane Ridge Revival (1800) lasted during the summers for a few years. But what were at first genuine manifestations of God's presence degenerated into fanaticism – nothing but shaking and jerking. There is a town in Kentucky called Shakertown, named for the 'shakers' who wouldn't admit the Revival was over.

And yet the *absence* of God's special presence can be most painful if the latter has been truly experienced. There are many ways it can be noticed. It may be as a result of leaving a place where God was powerfully present and returning to a church where no one has the slightest idea of what you felt. It may be going back to the same place where – last time you were there – God had turned up powerfully, but not this time.

As I intimated above, it can happen privately. You can know God's presence powerfully yesterday – and can hardly wait for today – and God's special presence simply isn't there today. In March 1993 I was praying one morning in our living room. I had been going through an extremely painful time. I had been discouraged beyond any level I had known. I sought the Lord like any other day, only I was more desperate. God came. It was the most powerful sense of his presence I had known in years. The old Nazarene preacher affectionately known as Uncle Buddy Robinson used to talk about God 'dropping a chunk of honey in my soul'. That happened to me. It lasted all day. While it was at its height I was determined, if possible, to keep that presence. I looked high and low in my heart, mind, life and experience to see how I could keep this. There was a residue the following day but by the third day it had almost totally diminished. I tried for a day or two to tell myself it was like it was, but I came to terms with its absence.

Not that God left me – or was grieved (so far as I could tell). He just remained behind and I had to go looking for him. I do know that there was a lot in me that needed looking into. I have had to admit to a lot of bitterness I didn't know was still present. I could see a lot of ways that had become a habit that needed changing, particularly regarding my family life. I wanted the Dove to adjust to me. I can honestly say I would not take anything in the world for that special presence, and the correcting in my life that it led to.

Joseph and Mary were not aware of Jesus' absence at first. This to me demonstrates what I have referred to above: we carry on a while 'thinking' he is in our company. But then comes the pain of knowing that his special presence is not there after all.

Two close friends in the Florida Keys, who happen to be professional bonefishing guides, entered into a prayer covenant with me. I pray each day for a particular matter that each of them asked me to pray for, and they for me. In my case I asked them to pray daily for me to become more sensitive to the Holy Spirit. I am thrilled to know that every single day John Sutter and Harry Spear pray 'that R.T. will become more sensitive to the Holy Spirit'. It has made a profound difference in my life; I began to notice unusual changes needed in me in a matter of months. For one thing, I have been reminded of that curious verse (quoted once above): 'If I were hungry I would not tell you' (Ps. 50:12). It hit me powerfully one day that – by saying that – God *was* telling us he could be hungry! It was a hint to anyone who will accept it, 'If I am hungry, maybe I *will* tell *you.*' It is one of the ways God tests our earnestness. For those who take this verse on the surface, God never tells anybody he is hungry. So they never think again about it. But for those who will ponder this verse carefully comes a clear invitation to experience God where others never would. It connects to those words, 'Lord, when did we see *you* hungry or thirsty?' (Matt. 25:44).

There is a strain in Scripture I have called (for want of a better phrase) 'the divine tease'. It is when God says or does the opposite of what he feels – only to see our reaction. It is God's set-up test by which he sometimes disguises his presence and purpose at first in order to reveal our real feelings. The divine set-up is designed to reveal what we are. Paul Cain says that God offends the mind to reveal the heart. God is not learning anything new about us of course; it is to let us see for ourselves – and sometimes to let others see – what we really are.

Jesus did this to the two people on the road to Emmaus, acting 'as if he were going further'. When they urged him to stay with them, he did – which is actually what he wanted all along (Luke 24:28–9). Jesus did this when the disciples were alone in a storm on the lake; he came walking on the lake and 'was about to pass by them'. But they cried out to him, which was precisely what he wanted them to do (Mark 6:48ff). When Jacob wrestled with the angel, the latter said, 'Let me go, for it is daybreak.' But Jacob replied, 'I will not let you go unless you bless me' (Gen. 32:26). That is what God wanted, despite the words, 'Let me go.' It was a pivotal moment for Jacob. For the angel said, 'Your name will no longer be Jacob, but Israel, because you have struggled with God and with men and have overcome' (Gen. 32:28).

Many of us would have let Jesus carry on down the road to Emmaus or let him pass by on the water (assuming it was a ghost), or given in to the wrestling angel. Or assumed that if God were hungry he wouldn't hint otherwise. Recognising his presence begins with recognising his *ways*. 'They have not known my *ways*,' lamented God (Heb. 3:10).

This is why we should want to be more and more sensitive to the Spirit. For if this prayer is answered – and continues to be answered – we will more quickly recognise God's special presence and absence. It takes as much sensitivity to the Spirit to recognise his absence as it does his presence. For we cannot feel his absence unless we know his presence. And the more acquainted we are with his ways the more likely we will be to discern his absence, even if everybody else thinks he is powerfully present.

Only Samuel knew that King Saul was yesterday's man (1 Sam. 16:1). Samuel is a type of 'today's man' who recognises in which direction the Sovereign Redeemer is moving and then moves in that direction. You could not have told the rank and file of Israel that Saul had lost the anointing of the Spirit. He wore the crown. He had the glory and prestige. He also had the following. He had the gifts – even continuing to prophesy (1 Sam. 19:23–4)!

Saul wore the crown but lost the anointing (1 Sam. 18:12); David had the anointing without the crown (1 Sam. 16:13). He developed a great sensitivity to the Spirit (cf. 1 Sam. 24:5), which helped partly to ensure that he would not succeed before he was ready.

Many of us are fooled by fanfare, hype, big crowds, oratory, lively worship and people being excited. I watched a man pray for people in my own church (it wasn't our service, he was only using the premises) and he preceded his 'prophecy' – 'word of knowledge' – with the words: 'No hype, no hype – just watch God work!' But it seemed to me that it was nothing but hype. The greatest freedom is having nothing to prove. This means that one doesn't have to make any claims at all if God really is at work. Shouting, 'No hype, no hype' is the same as 'protesting too much', as Shakespeare put it. Claims of Revival and God being spectacularly at work have caused many sincere people of God to think the Spirit was truly at work. A close examination of so many of these claims leads one, sadly, to conclude that God is in fact quite absent. Chapter 8, 'Pigeon religion', touches on this sort of thing.

What separates true religion from natural (or fleshly) religion is: who initiates what you do. 'Unless the LORD builds the house, its builders labour in vain. Unless the LORD watches over the city, the watchmen stand guard in vain' (Ps. 127:1). We can build a superstructure of wood, hay and straw – and some will think that it is a building made of gold, silver and precious stones (cf. 1 Cor. 3:11–15). But it is only a matter of time before one will say, 'God wasn't in it at all.' So the ancient prophet put it,' "Not by might nor by power, but by my Spirit," says the LORD Almighty' (Zech. 4:6). In this case the prophet meant *natural* might, *fleshly* power; it is that which has but a natural explanation at the end of the day.

The worst thing that can happen to any of us is to be deceived. 'And many false prophets will appear and deceive many', said Jesus (Matt. 24:11). Paul spoke of God sending 'a powerful delusion' so that some people would 'believe the lie' – all because they refused to love the truth (2 Thess. 2:10–11).

I was named after my father's hero, Dr R.T. Williams. When Dr Williams would preach the ordination sermon to new candidates he would counsel, 'Honour the blood, and honour the Holy Ghost.' By 'honour the blood' he meant we must preach the cross of Christ, the atoning blood, and never underestimate how much God honours his Son's blood. 'And honour the Holy Ghost.' By this he meant having the discernment to recognise his presence, to be willing to give in to the Spirit whenever he showed up in a special way. If necessary, forget your sermon and allow God to work.

I once saw this happen. When I was a teenager an evangelist came to our church in Ashland, Kentucky. He preached every night for two weeks. Every evening seemed better than the one before, every sermon a little more powerful. Crowds increased, expectancy was at a height. Then came the final service. I remember sitting on the front row – I could take you to the very spot. All eyes were fastened on the visiting preacher as he took his text. After he read it, he said nothing. There was quiet. Tears filled his eyes. He began singing a chorus I've known all my life:

> Wonderful, wonderful, Jesus is to me;
> Counsellor, Prince of peace, Mighty God is he;

Saving me, keeping me, from all sin and shame
Wonderful is my Redeemer, praise his Name.

My reaction was disappointment. 'Is he only going to lead us in singing?' I wondered. There was quiet. Then he proceeded:

Wonderful, wonderful . . .

By this time I was getting annoyed. Even as a teenager I wanted to hear his sermon. But he never preached. As he sang that chorus for the third time, dozens spontaneously got up out of their seats and *ran* to the altar, falling down sobbing and praying. I will never know what that sermon would have been like. I only know now that he was following R.T. Williams' counsel: he honoured the Holy Ghost rather than deliver his sermon.

When you have been in services like that it is easier to discern God's absence. When you have seen the Spirit truly work, you can also more easily detect the flesh at work.

It is therefore as essential to recognise God's absence as it is his presence. This way we are spared of getting on a bandwagon that will lead us to disillusionment.

In order to come to terms with God's absence, we must see the signs that this is the case. How then do we recognise his absence? It is often difficult to tell the difference between cause and effect: which comes first, the chicken or the egg? But it seems to me that what I have chosen to list below are sobering proofs that the Dove has *already* fluttered away.

Anxiety

Mary revealed her anxiety when she said, 'Your father and I have been anxiously searching for you' (Luke 2:48).

We have all been like that, even in the presence of God; but not in his special presence – when the Spirit is *at home* in us. Ungrieved.

That is truly the way it is in his special presence. It is a peace that 'transcends all understanding' (Phil. 4:7). It is God's own peace. This is different from peace *with* God (Rom. 5:1) which assures us that we are his and are accepted. And that, of course, brings peace. And yet there is even more than that which is promised: the peace *of* God. It is that alone which transcends all understanding: 'You will keep in perfect peace him whose mind is steadfast, because he trusts in you' (Isa. 26:3). This is why Paul counselled, 'Do not be anxious about anything' (Phil. 4:6), which seems ridiculous – until one has experienced it.

This is exactly what I lost in those days I have referred to above. It hurt to admit it. There was a time when I could literally feel peace inside my chest. I put it that way because it was virtually a physical feeling. Inner rest. No anxiety whatever. No fear. Just calm inside. It was extraordinary. I had to be honest with myself later and admit, 'It's not there.' I even tried to get it back by re-living it, or by telling it to some close friend. It was pleasant to talk about, but it didn't bring it back.

God has not given us a 'spirit of fear' (2 Tim. 1:7 AV), which best describes anxiety. One possible difference between fear and anxiety is that you probably know what you fear, but anxiety – a spirit of fear – is a general state of mind when you can't put your finger on what you are afraid of. It is what almost certainly emerges in our hearts when God's special presence subsides. It is precisely because Christ's special presence is available to us that Paul could say, 'Do not be anxious about anything' (Phil. 4:6), or 'Let nothing move you' (1 Cor. 15:58). For when that sweet anointing settles on us, our problems disappear; as 'Like a river glorious' has it,

> Not a blast of hurry touch the spirit there.

The experience I had on October 31st 1955 was preceded by a most dreadful anxiety. I felt panic as I prayed and prayed. Then two verses came into my head: 'Casting all your care upon him, for he careth for you' (1 Pet. 5:7 AV), and 'My yoke is easy and my burden is light' (Matt. 11:30). The latter verse certainly *didn't* describe me. I pleaded for grace to cast all my care – anxiety – on the Lord in the hope I might be able to say, 'My yoke is easy and my burden is light.' God came and the peace was incredible.

Irritability

'Son, why have you treated us like this?' his mother asked (Luke 2:48). She was clearly annoyed. Annoyed with herself she may have been, but irritated she was. Whenever we are in this agitated state, it is a dead give-away that the Dove has flown away or, as in this case, the Lord stayed behind. Once the Spirit withdraws his special presence, we are in a sense left to ourselves; our natural capabilities manifest and, almost certainly, irritability will be one of them.

When I was in my old denomination which held to the doctrine of entire sanctification, I was told that being sanctified wholly meant that the carnal nature was removed. A proof of this was that I would not lose my temper. But when different people *did* lose their tempers around me there was a loophole: Jesus' anger in the temple (John 2:15). It was called righteous indignation. Therefore when anybody manifested irritability it could be called righteous indignation. It might be said this was what Mary showed.

I doubt it. Mary lost presence of mind and showed herself to be thoroughly human like the rest of us. This does not justify her annoyance. As I said above, it is to her credit that she told Luke this story, making herself vulnerable. And yet it goes to show how we are when the Dove is not calmly perched on us. For when that special presence of the Spirit governs us, we are more likely to be in control of our words.

Love is not 'easily angered', said Paul (1 Cor. 13:5). This shows we can still get annoyed when there is love, but not easily. We are not impervious to mistreatment but we are less likely to react negatively when we are filled with the Spirit.

My point is this. When we are irritable we should take it as a sign we have been left to ourselves, as it were, and consequently must call out to God for mercy in order to find grace in this time of need. For once we begin speaking in an agitated state, it will come out wrong every time! Dr Lloyd-Jones once gave me this advice: 'When you are agitated, don't speak.' If we see irritability as a red light and stop, we can be spared regret. If we face our irritability and refuse to utter a word, there is the hope that, mercifully, the Dove will return and with him presence of the Spirit's mind: love that casts out fear (1 John 4:18).

Confusion, or muddled thinking

When his parents saw Jesus they were astonished and asked, 'Why have you treated us like this?' They accused Jesus of treating them in an unfair manner because he stayed behind in Jerusalem. They took it personally. They focused on themselves.

Joseph and Mary panicked, and this always means unclear thinking. The Holy Spirit always thinks clearly, and when we are Spirit-filled we will reflect clear thinking. We will not take rejection personally or see ourselves as the centre of what is going on. The Holy Spirit is self-effacing, speaking 'only what he hears' from the Father (John 16:13), just like Jesus (John 5:19).

God never panics. The degree to which we have the mind of the Spirit will be the degree to which we reflect his calm and gentleness. Clear thinking will demonstrate sound judgment, wisdom and also truth in doctrine. 'If anyone chooses to do God's will, he will find out whether my teaching comes from God or whether I speak on my own' (John 7:17). The ungrieved Spirit in us is the greatest preservative against theological error. Panic throws our thinking about biblical truth into disarray and, sadly, we sometimes foolishly defend propositions that have no warrant in Scripture as a result. There is therefore a close connection between our personal relationship with the Holy Spirit and what we believe. If we come to the calm that characterises God himself, we will be led to truth.

It is an awful feeling to be left to ourselves without the aid of the Spirit. It has happened to me – publicly. In our church's greatest crisis many years ago I was conducting a church meeting in which my leadership was under question.

I was not prepared for what was being said. I allowed the meeting to get out of hand and those who opposed my ministry got the upper hand. Nothing that came out of my mouth was inspired. I never felt so deserted. As people left the meeting – some with a look of glee on their countenances – I knew I had failed to demonstrate presence of the mind of the Spirit.

I was all right the next day. Clear thinking returned and I was able to anticipate even greater challenges soon coming. Why did the Lord 'stay behind' the night before? I do not know. But I learned not to pretend that I had the mind of Christ when I didn't. It taught me to know that the absence of clear thinking is the absence of God's special presence.

Not recognising the little foxes that spoil the vines

Here I refer to that curious verse in the Song of Songs, 'Catch for us the foxes, the little foxes that ruin the vineyards, our vineyards that are in bloom' (S. of S. 2:15). Before I bring this chapter to a close I want to share by way of personal testimony a little bit more of what I have learned about grieving the Spirit. I do this with the hope this will help someone to avoid unnecessary pitfalls that indicate the withdrawal of God's special presence. I list things that I now pray about all the time. For I have learned some of the things that grieve the Spirit in my own life. The following point to the likelihood that God is absent insofar as his special presence is concerned.

Self-pity Feeling sorry for ourselves always seems right at first. But it will never do to give in to it if we cherish the presence of the Dove.

Self-righteousness   This is the identical twin of self-pity. We reflect on our obedience and fancy that God is giving us a little pat on the back. Before we know it we let our left hand know what our right hand is doing (Matt. 6:3). The Dove leaves.

Defensiveness   This is not merely being 'touchy'; it is the natural instinct to resist any criticisms. It is the opposite of turning the cheek (Matt. 5:39). Love is partly 'letting be'. It is letting another point the finger at us and keeping quiet about it. It isn't easy, but the thought of losing God's special presence is sufficient motivation to let people say what they will.

Seeking a compliment   'Let another praise you, and not your own mouth; someone else, and not your own lips' (Prov. 27:2). I know what it is to hint for a bit of praise, especially after having to make a hard decision or after preaching a sermon. I recall once how I yearned to know, 'How did I do?' and tried very subtly to angle for a little feed-back – and inwardly I felt God's special presence subside. He knew what I was doing even if others didn't. Although they probably did.

Listening to gossip   I am not sure which is worse: telling another 'the latest' or listening to it. It isn't easy not to listen, especially if it is delicious bad news about one we find threatening. But it so easily grieves the Holy Spirit.

Talking too much   'When words are many, sin is not absent, but he who holds his tongue is wise' (Prov. 10:19). John Wesley would say that for every hour we spend talking we should spend two hours in prayer! I only know how easy it is to begin in the Spirit and end up in the flesh (cf. Gal. 3:3) when in conversation. At some point the Dove slips away and we are coping as if alone.

Rushing Getting in a hurry – what Joseph and Mary did – is almost always to move ahead of the Spirit. The Holy Spirit is not in a hurry. 'This is what the Sovereign LORD, the Holy One of Israel, says: "In repentance and rest is your salvation, in quietness and trust is your strength, but you would have none of it" ' (Isa. 30:15).

Pointing the finger 'Do not judge, or you too will be judged' (Matt. 7:1). This is invariably keeping a record of wrongs (1 Cor. 13:5) and, I can tell you, will result in the Spirit's special presence almost certainly departing before we finish a negative sentence.

When we honestly come to terms with the absence of God's special presence we are more likely to be in a fit state to find him. But when we justify things – simply because it is easier to presume God is with us – it hints of pigeon religion.

8

Pigeon religion

Are you so foolish? After beginning with the Spirit, are you now trying to attain your goal by human effort? (Gal. 3:3)

Pigeons and doves are in the same family and look much the same. But the pigeon is not the symbol of peace, neither was it a pigeon that came down and remained on Jesus. The turtle-dove, the dove that symbolises the Holy Spirit, is apparently different from pigeons in some interesting ways.

It seems to me that many claims to the presence of the Dove among us are but pigeon religion. By this I mean the counterfeit Holy Spirit. I certainly don't want to be unkind: I am very conscious of my own haste in presuming the presence of God – when it was not the Dove after all – too many times. It has often been a pigeon, not the Heavenly Dove, that gave me a 'religious' feeling.

As I mentioned earlier, I am indebted to my friend Pete Cantrell, who is an experienced expert in the area of pigeons and turtle-doves. His observations both amused me and gripped me. Their relevance for this book is almost astonishing. 'Do you see that pigeon there?' he said to me.

'Watch him, he's getting ready to bully the pigeon next to him who is perched on the spot he wants for himself.' I watched it happen seconds later. 'I don't see that happening with turtle-doves,' Pete added. 'Doves don't fight.'

I therefore pondered the difference between pigeons and doves as Pete spoke. I now wish to apply them to my own observation of certain aspects of church life and mistakes I have made.

A pigeon might look very like a dove at first

If you examined the cover of this book, did you notice that the birds flying in the background are pigeons? The white dove is obvious, but how many will notice the pigeons?

My wife Louise and I spend most of our holidays in the Florida Keys. Doves and pigeons there are common. One of my favourite areas to fish is next to a very small island called Dove Key, so named because doves love to nest there. Because that is its name, you expect to see doves there and assume that is what you see when you get fairly close. This is because one is preconditioned to see doves. But pigeons are there too!

When one is preconditioned for a certain manifestation of the Holy Spirit, it is easy to presume the presence of the genuine Holy Spirit when you see that particular manifestation. Take falling down and laughing as an example. Now I happen to believe that God has truly turned up in some places and the phenomenon of falling down and laughter is sometimes one of the authentic results. But when one goes to a church where this has happened a lot the expectancy is so high that one could easily fall to the floor after being prayed for, but there be an entirely natural explanation for it. A 'pigeon' coming down could get a similar result!

I once stood in a queue several years ago to be prayed for. The preacher asked all church leaders to come forward. I was sitting on the front row so I felt I had to go! And yet I was still sincerely hoping God would come down on me and do whatever he pleased. I estimate that seventy or eighty men and women were prayed for before the preacher got to me. Every single one of them fell backwards into the arms of the waiting 'catcher'. Then the preacher came to me. I stood there like the Statue of Liberty. Nothing happened. He prayed again, then a third time. Had I closed my eyes and been less conscious of standing straight I suspect I too would have fallen. I felt sorry for the preacher who prayed, and I wanted to apologise lest he felt embarrassed because a good number of people were watching to see if I would fall. I wanted to – I promise you. But I didn't want to be pushed over by a pigeon, either! I can get a pigeon to come down on me (when I have breadcrumbs) at Trafalgar Square any day of the week. I'm not saying that the Dove did not come down on some, if not all, of the others on that day. But I am saying that the expectancy was so high and the preconditioning so powerful that a pigeon may well have done the same thing.

This kind of thing can happen whenever God genuinely shows up in power. On one night there may be a most awesome sense of God. You feel it in the worship. In the preaching. In a time of prayer ministry. There are tears of joy and repentance, laughter and crying. People are apparently converted. Some are healed. You can't wait for the next night. It is the same worship group which leads in similar songs and hymns. The same preacher who takes his text from God's word. But God chooses not to show up. The question is, will the minister in charge have the integrity not to manipulate? Or does one have to make it appear to be like the previous night? If so, it is likely to be pigeon religion.

The genuine Dove is like the wind that blows 'wherever it pleases' (John 3:8). If one is truly sensitive to the Spirit, he or she must flow with the Spirit as well. But if one is equally sensitive to his absence, that person will honour God's sovereignty and not pretend. It takes a lot of courage to yield to the Spirit when he comes in power; it takes equal courage to be unpretentious when he is absent. Both aspects of the Dove can threaten one's comfort zone.

Moreover, there is nothing like a vast crowd to give the feeling of the Dove. For a high number of people will often create expectancy. Nothing preconditions a leader or a congregation like a filled church. If there is a lack of discernment and sensitivity to the person of the Spirit – which is needed all the more at such a time – a pigeon could come down on the heads of everyone present and no one would know the difference. I fear this has happened many times – and to the best of people.

The initial similarity of appearance between a pigeon and the Dove can even produce a 'bandwagon' effect – everybody being excited and wanting to be 'in' on what is happening. This can go on for a while. But eventually you wake up and come to terms with the sobering possibility that it was all hype. It hurts when you realise you were taken in. And that there was a very fleshly explanation for it all.

This can happen at an individual level as well, whether it

be speaking in tongues or prophetic words of knowledge. If we convince ourselves that God *must* manifest himself, we settle for almost anything. It is almost as though one says, 'Well, if I can't have the Dove I'll take a pigeon.' Even if these very words haven't been used, this is what is implied. For I have heard one say, 'I'd rather have wild fire than no fire.' I sympathise with that sentiment to some extent. For I too am tired of so much form of godliness without power. Traditional liturgy can be pigeon religion too! But if we believe that Jesus Christ is the same yesterday, today and for ever, we ought not to settle for the counterfeit.

A pigeon will easily adjust to us

A pigeon can be domesticated, trained and manipulated. A pigeon can be easily controlled and made to conform. Not a turtle-dove. 'The wind blows wherever it pleases. You hear its sound, but you cannot tell where it comes from or where it is going. So it is with everyone born of the Spirit' (John 3:8). True conversion is a sovereign act of God. You cannot make the Holy Dove do anything, unless it would be to fly away.

Perhaps one of the greatest abuses of the Spirit is some-times seen at this point. When we begin to feel we can control the will of the Holy Spirit we may be sure that pigeon religion has moved in. But we tell ourselves some-how this must be the Dove.

The issue: control. Who's in charge? I fear that some people play with the Holy Spirit as if he has no will of his own but will do what we tell him. We can fall prey to this when we are praying alone, and a powerful leader (even a worship leader or preacher) can sometimes control a crowd.

When I am alone praying I can quench the Spirit by doing all the talking. I can read the Bible and do all the thinking. The Dove does not have a chance to slip in – he is too much of a gentleman, in any case. So too with public leadership. One can control a crowd by his or her gift and personality. The people out there may not have a clue they are being manipulated.

The problem is, one's gift is in a sense also one's anointing. God shaped the gift and personality for his glory. It does not follow, however, that everything done by those who have an anointed gift is Spirit-led. We are under a solemn obligation to follow – not to lead – the Holy Spirit. Likewise I may have an anointing generally, but that does not mean that all I do is immediately and freshly anointed. I may have an anointing to teach and preach, but I can get ahead of the Lord, as Joseph and Mary did. When I do, pigeon religion takes over. The reason: I am in control.

I talked to a worship leader some years ago about his style of leading worship. He admitted he had a gifting that could control an audience and make them do almost anything – clap, jump, sit or weep. The people would never know they were like trained pigeons. It is an exceedingly rare worship leader who is utterly sensitive to the Dove and does not get ahead of the Lord.

In 1963 I was pastor of a church in Carlisle, Ohio. I read in the newspaper that a Christian minister (written up in *Time* magazine) who was a leader in the Glossolalia Movement was coming to Middletown, Ohio, less than ten miles away. (What used to be called 'Glossolalia', from the Greek word *glossa*, 'tongue', is now usually called 'Charismatic'.) So I went to hear him. Meeting him before the service he told me he was a real Calvinist[7] who spoke in tongues. That interested me. At the end of the service I stayed behind for prayer. I knelt at the altar and prayed, 'Lord, if this is from you, let it come; if not, stop it.' That is all I said. But I meant it.

The man prayed for me to receive the gift of tongues. But nothing happened. He then asked me to take literally the words, 'Make a joyful noise unto the Lord.' I wasn't sure what that meant. He said, 'Just make a joyful noise.' I was feeling a bit strange by this time. 'Just make a noise,' he continued – feeling a bit impatient, I thought. 'I don't understand,' I pleaded. 'Just say, "Ah." ' The pressure on me to speak in tongues was now so intense that I burst into a nervous fit of giggles – which the dear brother took to mean that the Holy Spirit had come. He hadn't. I was only laughing nervously. I felt manipulated once I didn't meet his expectations. Pigeon religion.

On the other hand, I do believe that some people (whom I know well) have indeed truly received the gift of tongues by being gently led by a godly person – sensitive to the Spirit. The problem was, I probably wasn't ready. And I doubt the Dove was, either. I know I was open at first but not at the end. Had the Christian leader who claimed he was a Calvinist (that he believed in the absolute sovereignty of God) been sensitive to the Spirit the fiasco could have been avoided. It put me off for a good twenty years.

Pigeon religion is man in control. It is manipulative, usurping the place of the Dove. The gracious Spirit is gentle and prudent. Like the meek and lowly Jesus, the Dove is neither intrusive (coming when not invited) nor obtrusive (unpleasantly noticeable). He is self-effacing. When he is invited and accepts the invitation the result is man out-of-the-picture. People will therefore want to wait and worship and let the Spirit do the leading. I fear it doesn't happen all that often, but when it does happen it is unforgettable. And worth waiting for.

The Holy Spirit will not be manipulated. The Dove flutters away as soon as one tries to do this, and the pigeon comes in.

Pigeon religion is territorial

A pigeon thinks a certain place belongs to him. Pigeon religion is manifested when we instinctively feel we have a 'corner' on the anointing. This is not only when we take ourselves too seriously but also when we fancy that we have the franchise on God's enterprise in a particular area, theologically and sometimes even geographically. The result is that we don't want another elbowing in on our calling, on our area of expertise or on our following.

It is the party spirit, a rival or competitive spirit. If we ourselves uphold a particular emphasis we sometimes want to be the sole vanguard for the 'party line'. Now we expect this in partisan politics, when a political party champions an issue that has been neglected. In such a case a particular political party wants to be the first to stress a special issue – whether it be the environment, social justice or lowering taxes. Therefore a politician resents it when a rival party wants to take the same line, even if in a different way. This is often seen when a party – whether known to be on the right or the left – moves towards the centre. Politicians are territorial.

Nothing is more deadly than a rival spirit in the Church of God. Take the subject of Revival, for example. I think we all generally agree that there is a heart-cry for Revival nowadays. I doubt there is any evangelical group or church that is not praying for Revival – a sovereign outpouring of God's Spirit that will revive the people of God and result in many conversions.

The problem here is, we all want it to come to *us*! We all tend to see ourselves as having 'borne the burden of the work and the heat of the day' (Matt. 20:12). We resent it if God would make others 'equal to us'! We want God to bless *our* efforts, *our* party line, *our* denomination or group. We therefore tend to dismiss out of hand any report of God coming down powerfully on anyone but *us*. We honestly believe it couldn't happen to those who are of a different theological persuasion or ecclesiastical setting.

Not long ago a weekly prayer meeting on the second floor of a civic centre in Nairobi centred on Revival. A group of a dozen Western missionaries prayed earnestly that God would send Revival to Nairobi. At exactly the same time 700 Kenyans were praying noisily and worshipping God – and growing rapidly – in the large auditorium just beneath them. The irony is, God was answering the missionaries' prayers! But they could not bring themselves to recognise Revival under their noses, for the Kenyans below them didn't represent their party line. Pigeon religion.

None of us has a monopoly on the anointing. Jesus' disciples wanted to stop someone praying in Jesus' name 'because he is not one of us'. Jesus stepped in: 'Do not stop him . . . for whoever is not against you is for you' (Luke 9:49–50). It is a reminder that we should rejoice over, not resent, someone praying in Jesus' name who isn't quite in our own group. Even Joshua, when he was young and still had a lot to learn, was unhappy when certain people were prophesying without recognised credentials. 'But Moses replied, "Are you jealous for my sake? I wish that all the LORD's people were prophets and that the LORD would put his Spirit on them!" ' (Num. 11:29). That is the way God wants us all to reject pigeon religion and pray for the restoration of God's honour in the world – not just on our small ministry.

Pigeon religion easily creeps into denominational journals and party-line magazines. Each tends, understandably, to uphold the party line. We have our own in-house magazine at Westminster Chapel. But if I ever allow any article to attack a servant of Christ – whatever their party line – it will not be under the anointing of the Dove. 'Doves don't fight each other,' says my friend Pete. But pigeons do. Any personal attack upon a fellow believer is almost certainly not under the leadership of the Spirit of God. As my old Kentucky friend C.B. Fugett used to say, even if crudely, 'The God in me will not fight the God in you.' This means that the Holy Spirit will not attack himself: namely, another person who is sincerely following Christ, or a movement that clearly desires to uphold the honour and name of God.

Usurping the privilege that belongs only to the Spirit

This means stepping in where I don't belong. It is elbowing in on the Spirit's territory. It is the Spirit who will do his work when I don't get in the way; that is, when I am but the channel of the Spirit. But when I try to do what he does best, he flutters away.

It can happen in the pulpit. I'm sorry, but I have made

this mistake too often in some forty-five years of preaching. It is when I have a person in mind as I preach and try too hard to make sure this or that person will get the point. It borders on preaching at the people.

There are five possible positions in this connection: (1) preaching *down* to the people – which is patronising them; (2) preaching *up* to the people – which is when I am intimidated by them; (3) preaching *for* the people – which is to entertain; (4) preaching *at* the people – which is cowardice; and (5) preaching *to* the people – which is what one is supposed to do. But when I preach at the people I am abusing my privilege and forfeiting the release of the Spirit's power on them. I am taking advantage of the platform God has given me. The people out there are helpless when I do that, and the result is the folly of the flesh.

As someone has said: the pulpit is no more the preacher's own platform than is the Communion Table his. When I conduct the Lord's Supper I must be sure I am focusing upon Christ and his death and all that we are to be in feasting upon him at the Supper. I dare not presume to abuse this responsibility. So too when I preach. The pulpit is the Spirit's platform, and when I get personally involved I compete with what is his sole prerogative.

It has been my lot more often than not in my preaching to find that the very people I hope will be present will be absent when I think I have a word they need. And should those people *be* present, they are usually the last to apply the word to themselves! But when I forget who is present and how the word might be applied, God will often apply that word powerfully. The people can usually tell in any case when it is truly God who is speaking to them. If they sense I know it is for them, it is often counter-productive.

The same is true regarding the matter of vindication. Vindication – when God clears one's name – is what God does best. He is the expert in this – absolutely brilliant. But only if he can do it without our help. The moment we try to say what might make us look better the pigeon moves in on the Dove's territory. God promises to vindicate but he only vindicates the truth. If we have been maligned when standing for the truth it gets God's attention. 'It is mine to avenge; I will repay,' the Lord promised (Rom. 12:19; Deut. 32:35). The worst thing we can do is to take into our hands what God wants far more than we do. But when we start saying things that make us look good and our enemy look bad you can count on it – it is pigeon religion taking over.

It is possible to begin in the Spirit and end up in the flesh in more areas than merely bringing in the works of the Law, as certain Galatians did in their lives (Gal. 3:2–5). I can start out ministering to another in the Spirit and before I know it get personally involved – in the pulpit, in prayer ministry or in the vestry. It can come from the unguarded comment, being too anxious to help or by being too desirous of wanting to look good. Pigeon religion sets in when I get in the way of the sensitive Dove who works but without competition. Barrie White used to say, 'The Holy Spirit is the only perfect preacher; he is the only one who never calls attention to himself.'

Anger in the presence of God

I've been guilty of this too. It is when I carry my resentment at 'what they did' and 'how could they do it?' right into my quiet time with God. Pigeon religion. The Dove is a thousand miles away but I tell myself the Holy Spirit is with me in my rash praying. Mind you, it is better to tell the Lord than to take it out on someone else. The psalmist said, 'I pour out my complaint before him; before him I tell my trouble' (Ps. 142:2). Therefore it isn't all bad to do this. The problem is when I begin to think the Holy Spirit is egging me on to feel as I do! And I fancy that he is as upset as I am. When I pray that God will punish them I am taking the low road. God tolerates me in this but isn't being honoured.

When at last I start praying that God will *bless* my enemy, I can immediately feel God say, 'That's better.' This is what he wanted all along. This is *always* the will of the Holy Spirit. Always. When my agitation persuades me that God is as angry as I am it is praying in the flesh. Sheer pigeon religion. It is my imagination.

We saw earlier that God sometimes teases us to believe what is the opposite of what he really feels – to test us. God did this with Moses. When the people of Israel were rebellious and not listening to Moses, God put a proposition to him: I will destroy this nation and start all over with you; Moses, what do you think of that? Here is the way God put it to Moses:

> 'I have seen these people,' the LORD said to Moses, 'and they are a stiff-necked people. Now leave me alone so that my anger may burn against them and that I may destroy them. Then I will make you into a great nation.' (Exod. 32:9–10)

I fear that, had I been Moses, I would have said, '*Yes!*' There have been times one could wish God would step in and wipe out certain people – for good. But Moses took a different line: '*No!*'

> But Moses sought the favour of the LORD his God.
> 'O LORD,' he said, 'why should your anger burn
> against your people, whom you brought out of
> Egypt with great power and a mighty hand? Why
> should the Egyptians say, "It was with evil intent
> that he brought them out, to kill them in the
> mountains and to wipe them off the face of the
> earth"? Turn from your fierce anger; *relent and do not*
> *bring disaster on your people.* Remember your servants
> Abraham, Isaac and Israel, to whom you swore by
> your own self: "I will make your descendants as
> numerous as the stars in the sky and I will give your
> descendants all this land I promised them, and it will
> be their inheritance for ever." ' Then the LORD
> relented and did not bring on his people the
> disaster he had threatened. (Exod. 32:11–14)

It is exactly what God hoped Moses would pray. It shows Moses' true greatness. Greatness is graciousness. Sir Winston Churchill used to say that the price of greatness is responsibility.

One of the easiest things in the world to do is to get too personally and emotionally involved in our own enterprise and forget it is God's work and reputation that matter – not ours. Anger in God's presence is understandable but is never right. When the Dove comes down the result will be our rising above ourselves and wanting God to bless and forgive our enemies. Anger will disappear and we will be filled with love and gratitude.

When my natural gift masquerades as the anointing

In *The Anointing: Yesterday, Today, Tomorrow* I referred to what some of us refer to as 'common grace', which Calvin calls 'special grace in nature'. It is sheer natural ability, but nonetheless a gift of God. It comes apart from regeneration (being born again). It is what enabled Artur Rubinstein to play the piano, it lay behind Rachmaninov's Piano Concerto in C minor, and Albert Einstein's great brain.

A Christian has it too. Common grace is God's goodness to all men and women. But when a Christian, especially a church leader, is highly gifted, that person could function admirably without much immediate help from the Holy Spirit. The Christian orators of this world with their sharp communicative skills have got to be exceedingly careful in this area. I suspect they could carry on before vast audiences without the anointing of the Spirit if they tried – and few if any could tell.

Such is not limited to oratorical powers, of course. A Christian who is gifted in making money could continue to do so without a fervent private prayer life. One could be a solicitor, physician, nurse or writer and be productive without having to forgive their enemies, graciously dignify trials or pay their tithes. Those looking on would never know whether the presence of the Dove is powerful in their private lives.

One great danger here is that one could deceive oneself. This is because the flow of God's special grace at the level of nature would seem so real that the person might say, 'God is truly with me or I would not be so good at what I do.' One may carry on towards Galilee and leave Jesus behind and never know the difference. The momentum of a natural gifting can go a long way. It is hard to reach or teach a person like this. They often can see little wrong in their lives if they are successful. It sometimes takes a severe tragedy – financial reverse, marriage or family breakdown, serious illness or accident – to get their attention.

When a gift of the Spirit masquerades as the anointing

It is harder to explain this one. But because the gifts of the Spirit are 'irrevocable' (Rom. 11:29), which means they are retained regardless of one's close walk with God, the manifestation of such gifts often serves to harden a person from listening further to God.

King Saul lost the special anointing (1 Sam. 16:1; 18:12) but continued to exercise the gift of prophecy. Indeed, on his way to kill David he began prophesying spontaneously (1 Sam. 19:23). His being consumed with hatred and jealousy over David apparently did not affect that gift of the Spirit one bit.

This is why Paul was concerned about the Corinthians. They thought that speaking in tongues proved that they were spiritual. 'Wrong!' says Paul, which is why he wrote 1 Corinthians 12 and 14 and thus called Love the '*most excellent way*' (1 Cor. 12:31). If one has the gift of tongues it can still be used despite bitterness and disobedience. It nevertheless is used by some as evidence that they are perfectly fine in God's sight. Pigeon religion.

One of the great mysteries of Samson's unusual anointing was that his weakness for women did not appear to diminish his strength at first. It was not until he told his secret to Delilah that he lost it all. Perhaps this helps explain how a Christian can seem to get away with sexual improprieties and carry on with apparent effectiveness. It is as though they flourish until they get caught! I know too many stories that illustrate this. It is scary. I don't understand it. But it indicates an insensitivity to the Dove before the stark truth is out in the open.

If one persists in such hypocrisy God will see to it that the whistle is blown, 'for God will judge the adulterer and all the sexually immoral' (Heb. 13:4). Our Lord demonstrated a lot of patience with sexual sin (John 8:1–11), but God nonetheless requires holiness among his people.

> It is God's will that you should be sanctified: that
> you should avoid sexual immorality; that each of
> you should learn to control his own body in a way
> that is holy and honourable . . . The Lord will
> punish men for all such sins, as we have already told
> you and warned you. (1 Thess. 4:3, 4, 6)

Pay day, some day. Such sin will be found out. And if this section should apply to someone involved in a relationship that is dishonouring to God – regardless of how your spiritual gift functions, I can only urge: break it off. Stop it. Fall on your face before God, confess it and turn from it. God will forgive (1 John 1:9) and the Dove will return as the pigeon is out of the picture.

A pleasant personality may look like the fruits of the Spirit

There are people who are just simply nice. They are sweet, friendly, cheerful and the type of person you want to be around with all the time. It is, however, just another aspect of God's common grace. Such people, possibly owing to their stable backgrounds and loving parents, manifest certain graces that put the oldest Christians to shame. But it may have nothing whatever to do with the fruits of the Spirit. They were that way before they were converted.

People like this, however, can be difficult to convince of their own need to show such fruits. Sooner or later their self-righteousness will surface if they haven't been convicted of sin. Smugness will sooner or later emerge, and if you recognise this in yourself I would urge that you thank God for your pleasing temperament, and pray harder than ever to be simultaneously sensitive to sin and the Spirit.

Emotional maturity can look like spiritual maturity

Some people grow up faster than others and some develop spiritually more quickly than others. There are many explanations for this. If someone has developed emotionally in a manner that shows fewer psychological problems, it should not be surprising that they *appear* spiritually mature as well. A person like this may or may not be strong in private prayer, worship and Bible reading, but will nonetheless appear level-headed and responsible compared to a neurotic Christian who prays all the time!

Regeneration and sanctification do not necessarily eradicate damaged emotions that come from abuse or neglect as one was growing up. For this reason a Christian who had severely damaged emotions as a child may struggle in areas that a relatively unspiritual person finds easy. The latter, however, may appear to be more godly when this may not really be the case. 'Do not judge, or you too will be judged' (Matt. 7:1).

The Dove, then, may not be the explanation for some people's apparent maturity. But they are often the ones who get voted into positions of church leadership; some go into the full-time ministry. They sometimes, not unlike King Saul, have the influence but not necessarily the anointing. If I may refer again to the recent poll which showed that the average church leader (vicar, pastor, church leader) only spends *four minutes a day* in quiet time, it should not be surprising if pigeon religion is widespread in the Church, speaking generally. The problem is complicated when so many ordinary Christians, sometime beset with emotional difficulties but nonetheless consumed with a love for God and his word, feel that their church leader isn't very spiritual.

Cultural and intellectual tastes can appear to be theological maturity

Some people obviously have a head start when it comes to upbringing. They are brought up with poise, elegance and a certain aptitude for things intellectual. They go to the better schools. They have a cerebral framework that some do not have.

When people like this become Christians they may take

165

to Pauline theology like a cat chasing a mouse. Does this mean they are more spiritual? Possibly but not necessarily. It could have a natural explanation.

People who are very theologically minded are not necessarily more interested in the things of the Spirit. They often think it is far more important to articulate the implications of justification by faith alone than to be personally filled with the Spirit.

At the other end of the spectrum, it is often the case that people who are more interested in teachings like the baptism of the Spirit are not very interested in the intricacies of theological orthodoxy. This likewise does not necessarily mean that they are more spiritual but, because they have not been trained in a certain manner, they are naturally attracted to experience more than to doctrine.

The temptation to judge the opposite of what appeals to us must be resisted strongly. What often has appeal has a natural rather than Holy Spirit motivated explanation.

In a word: pigeon religion may emerge in either case.

One final word on this matter: What I may wish to identify as pigeon religion may sometimes turn out after all to be God at work! I referred to Dove Key above. But there is also a small island called Pigeon Key – just under the seven-mile bridge between Marathon, Florida, and Key West. I suppose a dove may nest there too.

The truth is, we are all a mixture from time to time. Simon Peter was led by the Dove when he said to Jesus, 'You are the Christ, the Son of the living God.' For Jesus replied that this was not revealed 'by man, but by my Father in heaven' (Matt. 16:16–17). But several verses later, 'Jesus turned and said to Peter, "Get behind me, Satan! You are a stumbling block to me; you do not have in mind the things of God, but the things of men" ' (Matt. 16:23).

I have had to climb down from a strong public stand against this person or that group more often than I care to admit. For I have seen that what I may want to call a pigeon God may own as his Dove. Moreover, God can see a rough diamond – a stone nobody would initially suspect as real – and use it while the rest of us smugly uphold our own interest. The late Rolfe Barnard used to say, just before he went to Heaven, 'One day somebody is going to come along, pick up the Bible and believe it – and put the rest of us to shame.'

There is surely nothing worse than for God to reveal his glory – and we miss it. I repeat: you could never have convinced the ancient Pharisees, Sadducees or teachers of the Law that Messiah would show up – and they not recognise him. But it happened. An ever-increasing sensitivity to the Dove is the best guarantee that this mistake will not be repeated so often.

9

The road back

They went back to Jerusalem to look for him. (Luke 2:45)

The most natural thing in the world is to return to our comfort zone once we sense the anointing has been lifted. As soon as Joseph and Mary began looking for Jesus they sought him primarily among relatives and friends (Luke 2:44). Where else? Why look elsewhere? What other place would they have thought of? What other frame of reference would they know about?

But Joseph and Mary did not find him where they expected to find him. He simply wasn't there. They had to go back to the place where they lost him. But only because they were forced to do this; they had no other choice. They would never have made a 180-degree turn had this not been necessary.

What, then, are you and I to do once we come to terms with the loss of our anointing?

In this chapter we will examine the way back. The journey back to Jerusalem and finding the presence of Jesus involves important stages.

Repentance

The word 'repentance' comes from the Greek word *metanoia*, which literally means 'change of mind'. Joseph and Mary would not have thought a change of mind was necessary in their relationship with Jesus; they thought he was with them. They were wrong. They had to admit they were wrong.

Repentance partly means admitting, 'I was wrong.' We will never, never, never come to this unless we have to. Joseph and Mary only headed back to Jerusalem because they could not find Jesus. The natural inclination in all of us is to defend where we are and why. Unless we are forced out of our comfort zone we will stay in it.

Joseph and Mary had no choice. Like it or not, they were wrong to think that Jesus was with them. When they made a U-turn they were saying that they had been wrong in supposing Jesus to have been in their company. It took irrefutable evidence that he was nowhere near them to persuade them. When they couldn't find him, they made the U-turn. We are all like that.

God has to get our attention before we will repent. To admit to being wrong is the last thing on earth we want to accept. God gets our attention by making us see what we have lost. As long as we can feel we haven't really lost his special presence we are going to carry on.

We have seen that our natural gift – even supernatural gift – will often masquerade as the anointing. In a sense such a gift is the anointing. After all, our natural ability has a close connection to the divine calling. A special gift of the Spirit has got to be – in some sense – an anointing. This is partly why King Saul felt no great deprivation after Samuel's warning; he could still prophesy (cf. 1 Sam. 13:13 and 1 Sam. 19:23–4). I repeat: the gifts and calling of God are 'irrevocable' (Rom. 11:29).

As I said, this helps to explain how an evangelist or preacher can carry on in adultery and still preach with effectiveness. He feels no loss of power because he still functions with results. It often takes being *found out* – one way or another – before one is forced to admit to the truth.

There are two ways by which one is found out. First, they may get caught – exposed. Someone discovers the truth. Someone 'spills the beans'. The result is sometimes public shame. This is the way it sometimes happens, but I suspect it was often unnecessary at first. For God was almost certainly trying to get a person to see the truth in their heart all along. This brings me to the second way one is found out: you actually admit what is obvious, that the special presence is gone. Rather than continue as though nothing happened, you repent. But if such people do not repent God resorts to Plan B – public exposure. One then is on the spot. How deep the repentance is in this case is open to question. And yet one must not be too quick to question the validity of an unfeigned repentance because one got caught. King David apparently had no plans to repent until Nathan the prophet confronted him. David's repentance was genuine (2 Sam. 12:13). So God can use open exposure and confrontation to get a person's attention.

As for Joseph and Mary, they were certainly hemmed in. All knew the truth: Jesus wasn't with them. You would have to say they got found out – openly. It wasn't merely an inward feeling that Jesus was not with them. This was patently obvious to everybody who had been on the journey with them. It must have been somewhat embarrassing. In this situation we have no reason to believe God was dealing with them inwardly. But they were found out in any case.

To be granted repentance is a gracious mercy of God. It is being changed from glory to glory (2 Cor. 3:18 AV). It is when you discover new ways to please God, when a renewed measure of his presence shows our sin and forgiveness, and greater help in doing God's will; it is insight. The worst thing that can happen to a man or woman is to become stone deaf to the Holy Spirit, losing all sensitivity and thus being unable to be renewed any more to repentance (Heb. 6:6).

Therefore one should be exceedingly grateful that God succeeds in getting our attention in order to show our need to make a 180-degree turn in our lives. We should take any rebuke, discipline or chastening with both hands! 'Because the Lord disciplines those he loves, and he punishes everyone he accepts as a son' (Heb. 12:6). The word 'discipline' or 'chasten' (AV) comes from a Greek word that means 'enforced learning'. It is when we virtually have no choice but to take God's will on board. It shows not only that we are loved but that God isn't finished with us yet. Never forget this: whenever God chastens it means we have a future and that the best is yet to come!

The way back to Jerusalem is the way of repentance. It is admitting that we have lost the special presence of God. We have been wrong in our thinking and presumption.

Seeking God's face

Joseph and Mary went back to Jerusalem 'to look for *him*' (Luke 2:45). They were looking for a person. They were looking for one they knew they would recognise. No one else would do. A holy city Jerusalem may be, but there was only one person there they wanted to find. No comfort zone would do, no holy place would suffice. They wanted to find *him*.

I will get up now and go about the city,
    through its streets and squares;
I will search for the one my heart loves.
    So I looked for him but did not find him.
    (S. of S. 3:2)

One thing I ask of the LORD,
    this is what I seek:
that I may dwell in the house of the LORD
    all the days of my life,
to gaze upon the beauty of the LORD
    and to seek him in his temple. (Ps. 27:4)

When God hides his face he wants us to seek him. This is almost certainly one reason he hides his face – that we will go looking for him. He tests our earnestness to see what our reaction will be when he hides himself.

    The question is, will we recognise the difference between the flow of our natural gift and the flow of God's special presence? Will we notice the difference between those endowments that are bestowed via common grace and the anointing that has its origin in the radiance of his face?

Will we discern the difference between a gift of the Spirit – which is irrevocable – and the intimacy that kindles holy fire?

In a word: are we sensitive to the Dove? Will the counterfeit do? Never! It is only a matter of time until we will notice what we have lost when Jesus stays behind. And when we see this, our repentance must be followed by seeking his face. The U-turn is not enough. Some may feel it is sufficient accomplishment merely to admit we've been wrong. But that is only the beginning.

We therefore must go looking for Jesus. It may mean going not only outside our comfort zone but enquiring where we've never been. It wasn't enough for Joseph and Mary to go to Jerusalem. Once arriving there they still had to find *him*. Obviously he wasn't where they thought he would be, for they took three days to find him. As I said in Chapter 1, you can step out of a flowing stream but you can never step back in at the same place. For the flow moves on. They had to go where they hadn't thought necessary.

A familiar theology is also a very common comfort zone. So too with a familiar liturgy, clichés or style of worship. As I said, we almost certainly will begin to look for Christ in our comfort zone. But what if he isn't there? Will we admit to this too?

Seeking the face of the Lord is to settle for nothing but him. We must seek him until we find him. It may require examining teaching we had previously dismissed out of hand. It may mean associating with people we once said we'd have nothing to do with. It may be singing lines we previously felt had nothing in them for us. Those who have concentrated only on the things of the Spirit may have to go seeking God's word in a manner they never thought they'd have to do. Those who were at home with the word and the finer points of theology may have to submit to a ministry of prayer carried out by people they had once sneered at. Traditionalists may have to begin singing, 'Shine, Jesus, shine'; contemporary-style worshippers may have to seek God by singing 200-year-old hymns. Once God has succeeded in getting our attention we will have to repent and then carry through by seeking our Lord's face and not giving up until we find him. A lot of humbling, climbing down and sheer embarrassment may be part of the journey back.

Many years ago, shortly after we were married, Louise developed a condition in her jaw; she could barely open her mouth. A doctor said it would require fairly major surgery. We never knew what caused it; we only knew that she reached the stage where she could hardly chew but could only take soup without pain. In the meantime I met a man in Fort Lauderdale who had founded a rescue mission for tramps and beggars. He took in old furniture, fixed and sold it in order to support his mission. He lived by faith and hard work. I was so impressed with him that I asked him to come to our home for supper. The evening was thrilling as he told us of remarkable answers to prayer. He got up to leave at about eleven o'clock. As he headed to the door I told him about Louise's jaw. Without asking for her permission he simply put down his briefcase, placed his hand on her jaw and said, 'In Jesus' name be healed. Now open your jaw.' She did! She was healed on the spot. It seemed no big deal to him. He picked up his briefcase and went home.

That night taught me a lesson. Some people have an unusual anointing whose theology we would be uncomfortable with. I will not try to explain his theology, I will only say that it was rather weird. But he was also uneducated. I have learned across the years that God is often found where we have no intention of looking. But when we are desperate, all that can change.

A lesser-known person in the Bible is Jephthah. He had been rejected by the whole of Israel. But the time came when they were so desperate that they turned to him. He saved the day (Judg. 11:33) and is given mention in Hebrews 11:32. But he was the last person they wanted to give them help. God has a way of bringing all our options down to one – the last we wanted! It is part of God's sense of humour!

Seeking God's face means settling for nothing but the special presence of God – and not stopping until you know you have found him. Wherever he is.

Not giving up

'After three days they found him' (Luke 2:46). It took one day to lose Jesus; three days to find him. I will say it one more time: it is easier to lose the anointing than it is to get it back. But if it is the recovery of what we lost that we truly want, it is what can happen. God does not tease us, dangling a carrot to demoralise us.

> Do not be deceived: God cannot be mocked. A man reaps what he sows. The one who sows to please his sinful nature, from that nature will reap destruction; the one who sows to please the Spirit, from the Spirit will reap eternal life. Let us not become weary in doing good, for at the proper time we will reap a harvest if we do not give up' (Gal. 6:7–9)

Three days is a relatively short period of time in which to seek the Lord. But if we are to see the account of Joseph and Mary as a parallel it suggests that it could take three times as long to re-experience the special presence of God as it takes to lose it. This analogy must therefore not be pressed too far, as we will see in the next chapter. But we must be prepared to take as long as is needed to get back what we lost. Any effort or any amount of time is worth it.

My own return to Jerusalem has included more praying, occasional fasting, a return to tithing and not a few occasions of 'losing face'. I do not wish to presume what you may have to do in the event that you, like me, have experienced the withdrawal of the Dove. I will, however, share some of what I have had to do.

Dignifying the trial   I had planned to preach through James in the autumn of 1979. But I was haunted by the opening exhortation: 'Consider it pure joy, my brothers, whenever you face trials of many kinds' (Jas. 1:2). I had to square my lifestyle of being the world's greatest complainer with that verse. I couldn't. Something big needed to happen to me. But God taught it to me through a small thing – it is often his way.

I remember it as though it were yesterday. It was in Kissimmee, Florida, near Disneyworld. The previous year I had taken the family to Disneyworld and they wanted to go back. I was quite ready to agree, mainly because I knew I could return to a pizza shop in Kissimmee where I had eaten the most succulent, delicious pizza of my life! So on the day we checked into our motel in Kissimmee the following year we headed for the pizza parlour. Each of us ordered a pizza to our own taste; I myself got the 'works' –

everything that comes, including anchovies. The chef forgot our order somehow, and forty-five minutes later I let him know in a most articulate manner that I was not happy. It was his first day at work. But he finally called us to the front and handed us our pizzas and I paid without a smile. Just before we started back it began raining. Now when it rains in Florida, it rains! Although the motel was less than a mile away, by the time we parked next to our room there was almost a foot of water. Louise and the kids took their pizzas, and made a run for it. I opened my door, stepped in a foot of water, and opened the back door to get my pizza. The rain poured down on the brown paper bag that was holding it, and out came everything – anchovies, peppers, mushrooms, sausages, pepperonis – straight into a puddle of water. I reported my grievous loss to the family, who were digging into their pizzas, then headed back to the pizza parlour.

Something wonderful happened. I don't understand it, I can only say God was gracious. I thought of James 1:2: 'Consider it pure joy, my brothers, whenever you face trials of many kinds.' 'Either this is true or it isn't,' I said to myself. I made a decision then and there to dignify that little trial (although it seemed big at the time). I confessed my anger to God and promised I would, from then on, accept the smallest trial as a gift from him. To quote another verse from 'Like a river glorious':

Every joy or trial falleth from above,
Traced upon our dial by the Sun of love.
We may trust Him fully, all for us to do;
Those who trust Him wholly find Him wholly true.
(Frances Ridley Havergal, 1836–79)

The most wonderful peace came over me, the nearest I had experienced since October 31st 1955. I also went to that chef on bended knee, told him what had happened and that I would gladly wait for him to do another pizza for me. He didn't even charge me! But I can never forget those moments. The next day – all day long – at Disneyworld I was aglow with a great measure of renewal of the Spirit.

I tell this story because it taught me that we must adjust to the Dove in the smallest, though very difficult, episodes of life. To keep the Dove *remaining* is to adjust day and night to every relationship and circumstance.

Total forgiveness   We must not forget what Paul went on to say following Ephesians 4:30: 'Get rid of all bitterness, rage and anger, brawling and slander, along with every form of malice. Be kind and compassionate to one another, *forgiving* each other, *just as* in Christ God forgave you' (Eph. 4:31–2). The idea of forgiving others was – to me – head knowledge, I must admit. I also thought that in *my* case of being hurt and maligned, God not only understood but waived the rules. Wrong. What follows is given in more detail in some of my other books, especially *God Meant It for Good* (Paternoster). My old friend Joseph Tson said to me in what was at the time my darkest hour: 'R.T., you must *totally forgive* them; until you totally forgive them you will be in chains.'

It was almost certainly the hardest thing I've ever had to do. But the benefit so outweighed the carnal wish that my enemies would get what they deserved that I was never to be the same again. Talk about peace? It began to come back in waves as I eventually prayed not only for the forgiveness of those who hurt me but I actually prayed that they get away with it! After all, the Lord reminded me, have I not got away with a lot? Yes, a lot. When I measured what I had been forgiven, forgiving others became progressively easier. And another token, or taste, of peace that comes from the presence of the ungrieved Spirit flowed.

Walking in the light 'But if we walk in the light, as he is in the light, we have fellowship with one another, and the blood of Jesus, his Son, purifies us from all sin' (1 John 1:7). I have had to make a number of crucial decisions over the past twenty years that led to what I believe is a greater anointing than I have had before. Some of the events are described in *The Anointing: Yesterday, Today, Tomorrow*. I can only say here that in learning to dignify trials (great and small) and learning to forgive those who have hurt me, I believe God may well have put me to one side.

Walking in the light is to focus on Jesus and maintain the awareness of the gentle Holy Spirit as much as possible. I have a long way to go and I learn new lessons all the time. But I have been sobered by the essential factor: God doesn't bend the principles of the ungrieved Spirit for me. In a word: the Dove does not adjust to me, I have to adjust to him.

In addition to Paul's affirmation 'God cannot be mocked' (Gal. 6:7), at least twice God put it like this:

> But if from there you seek the LORD your God, you will find him if you look for him with all your heart and with all your soul. (Deut. 4:29)

> You will seek me and find me when you seek me with all your heart. (Jer. 29:13)

This means taking on board any warning, any 'new' light in

which to walk and any promise the Lord has given. Whatever we already know grieves the Spirit must be set aside
categorically if we want a renewal of his special presence.
Being prayed for by those who have a ministry of prayer
and laying on hands will do no harm, but whatever renewal
that may come from this will also wane rather soon if you
do not develop a sensitivity to the Spirit on your own.

The forgotten anointing is in part that which is experienced on your own and, almost certainly, by yourself – by
learning what makes the Dove feel at home with you. Get
all the prayer ministry you can. Sit under the best teaching
and preaching you can find. Worship with God's people all
you can. But at the end of the day the anointing that
characterises the Dove is tied to what you are as a person.
Day and night. At home or at work. With friends and with
family. At church or in solitude with Jesus. It is the forgotten
anointing.

Being prepared to recognise in Jesus what you hadn't seen before

'After three days they found him in the temple courts, sitting
among the teachers, listening to them and asking them
questions' (Luke 2:46). This was a Jesus they hardly knew!

Why? When we are away from the Lord, he moves on.
By the time we catch up with him he is not the same – to
us. He continues to work. We have not been in on it. We
therefore have to make new adjustments to what he is doing
at the time we rediscover him.

Many people who have opposed what God is doing – in
any generation – were not as close to the Lord at the time
as they thought. For if they had been, they would not have

been so slow to recognise him. It is when we move on without him – while he continues to manifest his glory elsewhere – that warps our discernment. 'All is yellow to the jaundiced eye.' Our sight of the Lord is often fixed in one direction – the way we knew him when we last felt his presence. But if we move on and he is at work elsewhere we must be prepared to bow to him – wherever he is working and whatever he is doing.

'In the temple courts.' That is the last place they looked for Jesus. I don't know where Joseph and Mary went first once they arrived back in Jerusalem. I only know this is the last place they looked. Had they come there first they could have been spared three days' anguish.

What I have been saying in this chapter is seen precisely here: the Lord is to be found in surprising places. And yet when you think about it for long, there isn't much surprising about it after all – especially if we know our Bibles, as well as a little bit of church history. God loves to surprise and astonish. But when he does this it soon becomes clear there is nothing unreasonable after all in the manner and place he chose to show himself.

'Sitting among the teachers.' Perhaps Joseph and Mary were a little hurt that he would do this without them. What an amazing sight to behold – their son sitting among the teachers. They would like to have been in on that. Why weren't they informed?

I have had to ask myself a hard question from time to time: when I see something unusual by a true servant of Christ that I hadn't experienced and hear depths of insight I myself hadn't come up with first, do I feel anger towards the Lord or gratitude that I have the presence of mind to see his sovereign hand at work? If I am angry (as Mary was), I betray how far I have moved ahead of the Lord. If I feel gratitude, I show I am walking in the Spirit – which is a wonderful place to be. I can rejoice in what God is doing apart from me for, after all, it is *his* glory I must want! I therefore have no right to resent what he is pleased to do, wherever it is or with whom. But if I rejoice in it, it is a good sign that I please the Lord.

'Listening to them and asking them questions.' Does it surprise us to whom the Lord listens? Do we fancy he only listens to us and those who hold our points of view?

God's elect are scattered all over the globe and made up of every tribe, people, tongue and nation. This means all cultures and unusual ways of worshipping Christ. It does not mean that I agree with them. It does not necessarily mean the Lord agrees with them. But he listens to them. He listens to my enemies! He loves them too. When he asks them questions we don't know their response. But he may well be in communication with them. It is the way they are going to change, should they need changing. I should therefore rejoice at any interaction between the Lord and those I may not be in close touch with.

Not being surprised over the effect the Lord has on those you have not been a part of

'Everyone who heard him was *amazed* at his understanding and his answers' (Luke 2:47). While he continues to work without us he dazzles people we never met. We should rejoice that this is happening. It is to the everlasting credit of the Jews who initially opposed Paul and Barnabas that they were 'very glad' once they realised Gentiles had been truly converted (Acts 15:3).

Those who heard Jesus in the temple, then, were 'amazed'. This is what Jesus always does. He amazes. He did it without Joseph and Mary. He does it all the time without you and me. When those outside our circles of influence are amazed at Jesus we should be very glad.

They were amazed at his 'understanding and answers'. These teachers in the temple courts were not prepared for what they heard. Jesus had a grasp of the things of God that moved them to the core of their beings. You can be sure they needed everything Jesus said. We do not pick up a hint of rejection but only amazement.

We should be thrilled over any report of Revival in any part of the world. And yet it is easier to rejoice in a movement of the Spirit in the Third World than across town. If I can praise God for what he is doing in Brazil or India, can I praise God for blessing on Holy Trinity Brompton, All Soul's Langham Place or Kensington Temple – especially if I'm not seeing the same blessing at Westminster Chapel at the moment?

What Joseph and Mary saw was right before their eyes. And it was their son at the centre of it all! They could not say 'That's not really God,' as you and I may want to do if we see something outside our comfort zone. They could not deny that they finally found Jesus. But they only focused on themselves. 'Why have you treated us like this?' (Luke 2:48).

That is about as insensitive as one can get. It goes to show how out of focus, though previously so close to Jesus, Joseph and Mary had become in their perception of him.

It can happen to us. The road back to the anointing must find us thrilled that we ever found our Lord again! We must accept him as he is and be glad for anything he is

doing wherever it is. Don't carp – just thank God you
found him!

10

The return to the anointing

See, I am doing a new thing! Now it springs up; do you not perceive it? (Isa. 43:19)

When his parents saw him, they were astonished. (Luke 2:48)

Once we discover we have moved on without the Lord – and apparently lost a measure of the anointing – our consuming passion is to recover what we once enjoyed. Nothing else really matters when you come to terms with the fact that things are not as they were.

Why must it take so long to return to the anointing? Must it always be true that it is easier to lose the anointing than it is to get it back? Why can't we just apply 1 John 1:9 ('If we confess our sins, he is faithful and just and will forgive us our sins and purify us from all unrighteousness') and be done with it? Won't God instantly forgive once we see that we have erred in moving ahead without Jesus?

Yes. But if that is so, will the anointing not return at once without our having to return to it? Yes, should God be pleased to grant it. For sometimes he does. Not all of my own experiences of grieving the Spirit are met with a long era of agony. Many, many times the Spirit's anointing returns in moments – in fact, *most* of the times that is what happens.

There are degrees to which we all move ahead without Jesus. For there are little ways and big ways we can forfeit the sense of God's special presence. We can do it by the unguarded comment or by carelessness in small matters, such as in less important decisions. I've done it by getting in the flesh in my preaching. When I come down from the pulpit and realise I said something that was unwarranted I confess it to God and learn from my mistake. I've had to fulfil invitations that I should not have accepted – and learn from my haste.

God is not looking over our shoulders with a magnifying glass to see what he can find that is wrong with us. For one thing he doesn't need a magnifying glass; all things are 'uncovered and laid bare' before his eyes (Heb. 4:13). He knows our frame and remembers that we are dust (Ps. 103:14). When we grieve the Spirit in smaller matters, it is true, yes, the Dove distances himself for a moment – he does us no favour not to do so. But he graciously comes alongside and shows us our folly that we might confess it and get on with things. Yet we should learn to 'break the habit', as Michael Eaton says, when we see ourselves continually moving ahead without the Lord in the less important things.

But must God hide his face from us for a great length of time when we have erred in a more serious manner? Not necessarily. It may well depend on us and our reaction to his having 'stayed behind'. In the case of Joseph and Mary, their reaction was anger. 'How dare he do this to us?' was virtually in their hearts when they discovered Jesus' absence – which came out when they finally found him (Luke 2:48).

188

Therefore one of the reasons it takes a while to return to the anointing is that we ourselves may need sorting out.

Take the case of sexual immorality, for example. This sin brings disgrace upon the honour of God's name probably like no other kind of sin. A greater measure of discipline may be necessary. How one reacts to the need of discipline may also be a factor. There are two possible reactions to 'getting caught'. One is to be sorry at once and not be defensive. This was David's reaction when Nathan the prophet confronted him (2 Sam. 12:13). David immediately sought the Lord, wrote Psalm 51 and was given assurance that he would be used again. 'Then I will teach transgressors your ways, and sinners will turn back to you' (Ps. 51:13).

The other reaction is not responding so graciously. Some dig in their heels and resent those who 'blow the whistle', and stay defensive. People like that are probably going to have to wait a long, long time before they can be restored. They should not blame God if this takes time.

There are therefore degrees to which we can move along without Jesus. If you have done this in a big way, (1) admit it, (2) don't be defensive, (3) turn the matter over to God, and (4) seek his face with all your heart. God will pick up things from where you are, this being true no matter how old you are or how deeply you grieved the Lord! God is a gracious God and will begin at once to cause all things to work together for good (Rom. 8:28). This is his promise!

The question is, do we ever truly recover exactly what we lost? I believe the honest answer is, both yes and no. Why should that be?

First, we are never fully prepared for the anxiety that accompanies our journey back to Jerusalem or for the sobering discovery of what the return to the anointing entails. For the journey back is fraught with anxiety and the fear we might not find what we lost. The three days of looking for Jesus must have seemed like an eternity to Joseph and Mary.

Second, we are never fully prepared for the way the anointing manifests itself once we find what we are looking for. When Joseph and Mary saw Jesus they were 'astonished'. Was it the same Jesus? Again the answer is, both yes and no. It was Jesus all right. There was no doubting it was he. But in another sense not the Jesus they knew! Never before had they seen him like this.

They were not altogether happy. They should have been relieved and thankful. But no. 'Son, why have you treated us like this? Your father and I have been anxiously searching for you' (Luke 2:48). For it seemed like a different Jesus to them. And so in a sense he was. But it was nonetheless the same Jesus.

The anointing to which we must return is virtually a *new* anointing. It is the new anointing to which we must all adjust once we find where it is and how it is manifesting. Adjusting to the Dove is a lifelong process of agony and surprise.

Some of us take longer in our return *to* the anointing because the whole time we are looking for the return *of* the anointing. We all are prone to say, 'The old wine is better.'

And no one after drinking old wine wants the new, for he says, 'The old is better.' (Luke 5:39)

We all tend to begin looking for the recovery of the anointing in our comfort zone but almost always end up discovering that the new anointing is indeed outside our comfort zone. When we return to that anointing we find God saying to us: 'See, I am doing a new thing!' (Isa. 43:19).

One of the reasons God stays behind and allows us to move on without him is that we will be forced to see the new and different ways he chooses to manifest his glory. Our first reaction is often the same as that of Mary and Joseph when they finally found Jesus; they were astonished. They wanted the Jesus they knew and were comfortable with. But they were never to have him exactly like that again.

I am reminded of my friend who chided me for some of the people I have invited to speak at Westminster Chapel. 'R.T., if Revival comes to London, I'll know it.' In much the same way I think many sincere, godly people in Wales continue to look for Revival to turn up there as it did under the powerful ministry of Evan Roberts in 1904–5. But that may or may not ever happen again in the same way.

> Do not say, 'Why were the old days better than
> these?'
> For it is not wise to ask such questions.
> (Eccles. 7:10)

When Mary Magdalene fell at Jesus' feet and held on to him, Jesus said, 'Do not hold on to me, for I have not yet returned to the Father. Go instead to my brothers and tell them, "I am returning to my Father and your Father, to my God and your God" ' (John 20:17). He was having to tell her as gently as he could, 'Nothing will be the same again.' For Mary was having to begin the difficult transition from the level of nature – the way she basically recognised Jesus – to the level of the Spirit, the new way to which she would have to get accustomed to recognising him.

The Christian life is a continual series of events that lead us out of our comfort zone. It is a matter of making repeated transitions from the natural level to that of the Spirit. The irony is that the new level of the Spirit will eventually become another comfort zone and that too will have to be left behind in some sense.

What Paul Cain calls 'no camping allowed' is relevant here. We break out of the old mould (no small breakthrough at the time) but then want to stay put. The pioneer becomes a settler. But this is not on for any of us in this life. Yes, our natural tendency is to 'camp' – to settle in. But no. We are called to follow the stigma of the Spirit until the day we die or the coming of the Lord. Jesus' disciples were never allowed to 'camp'.

It was no small thing for the disciples to leave their nets to walk with Jesus. But that was only the beginning. One stigma after another followed. Then came the biggest transition yet; Jesus said, 'I am going away' (John 16:7).

And I will ask the Father, and he will give you
another Counsellor to be with you for ever.
(John 14:16)

What had been pivotal early on – leaving their old jobs – had eventually become a settled-in habit. More battles were on the way. Jesus soon tried to get the disciples to see that he would be crucified. But they let that message go through one ear and out the other. Therefore when he died they were devastated. Then came his resurrection – which thrilled them. They then adjusted to his death. The forty days of Jesus' turning up and disappearing were further preparation for the coming of the Spirit. But even after the coming of the Spirit there would still be more challenges that kept catapulting them from each comfort zone to new levels of offence.

We will be allowed to become settlers in Heaven. Until then we must continue to adjust to the Dove and the surprising and unpredictable ways God challenges our faith. This too is called being changed from glory to glory (2 Cor. 3:18 AV).

If we have lost the anointing – to whatever degree – we must prepare ourselves for the unexpected ways God will be found. Like it or not, we can't go back. Those who keep going back and hoping, hoping, hoping they can have that old feeling they once enjoyed may even be looking for nostalgia more than the Holy Spirit.

All that I have tried to outline above is seen in some detail as we take a final look at the central story of this book. What did Joseph and Mary have to come to terms with? To what exactly did they have to adjust before they returned to Galilee with the Son of God?

Accepting that God may choose to work without our being in on it

This point, touched on earlier in this book, needs to be stressed because of the natural tendency in all of us to suppose we must always be 'in the know' as to what God is up to. The 'over-familiarity' with God that so often charac-terises people who spend a lot of time with him needs to be checked again and again for one's own good.

When we get to know God in some depth we often fancy we know him better than we really do, as I said. But what is worse, we want some control. It is so often true that the next step after being very 'in' is to want to control. It often happens in relationships. It also happens in our intimacy with the Lord. We feel 'in' and before we know it we feel we have some 'claim' upon God – that we must be informed by him of his every next move before someone else is told.

Joseph and Mary discovered that God was up to something without them – and when they found Jesus they were upset. They felt let down. I know I have felt that way again and again. I may know abstractly that God is 'wholly other', as the theologians say (which means he is utterly different in himself from all his creation). But to see him manifest himself in a way *other* than what I have been used to or heard of will often make me think, 'This can't be the God I know.' But it certainly can be him. He is wholly other and entirely sovereign and has the right to move in any direction without telling those who may think they are closest to him.

Seeing God do the new and different

Here was the twelve-year-old Jesus in the temple courts holding his own with the mature teachers of the Law. Sitting in a rabbinic position rather than like a child, then dazzling the experts, was unprecedented.

If one were looking for a biblical mandate or example to validate what Jesus was doing, one would be in difficulty. There simply was no established precedent, tradition or verse in the Old Testament that would put Joseph and Mary at ease. A common defence mechanism many of us use when we wish to reject a particular manifestation of the Spirit is to demand biblical precedent for such. Jonathan Edwards wrote *Religious Affections* because he faced charges that what was happening in his day had no biblical precedent. The truth is, part of the stigma is the *continuation* of God's surprises – from the shock of the cross to the bewilderment of God's latest way of offending us. Hebrews 11 is our precedent: not one person described was allowed to repeat the exact manner of obedience that preceded them. Hebrews 11 is, in a sense, still being written by us!

A pattern to be found in church history is one of finding those who thought they were 'closest' to God being the most astonished at what God is doing. This is often seen as a way to opt out with a good conscience. In fact that is precisely how the chief priests felt no guilt in crucifying Jesus. Isaiah saw it coming: 'We considered him stricken by God, smitten by him' (Isa. 53:4).

God himself, believe it or not, sometimes seems to allow a convenient way out for those who hope they don't have to embrace the latest movement of the Spirit. Whether it be those who say, 'Is this not Jesus, the son of Joseph, whose father and mother we know?' (John 6:42) and feel perfectly justified in what they reject, or those who find any respectable rationale that keeps them in their comfort zone, we all manage to avoid what is unpleasant and feel good about it. But this does not take God by surprise. It is as the psalmist put it, 'If I were hungry I would not tell you' (Ps. 50:12). The Holy Spirit is too much of a gentleman, it would seem at times, to intrude into our fears and biases.

Joseph and Mary were hemmed in and knew this was indeed their son – even if a somewhat different Jesus from the one they had been accustomed to. But they were also honoured to be on the spot. All who know what it is to be boxed into a corner like that should feel singularly blessed. I know what it is to be *forced* to see the truth of what I hoped wasn't true – and have to back-pedal. It is painfully embarrassing but a sign of God's magnanimous mercy. For he didn't have to show me the truth in the first place.

Having to go where the anointing is at work rather than wait for it to come to us

Going to Jerusalem wasn't enough; Joseph and Mary still had to find Jesus. Presumably it took a day merely to get back to Jerusalem, but Jesus had apparently moved to another spot. Finding him took another two days which meant a total of three days. He didn't come to them; they had to go to him and not give up until they found him.

When the Toronto phenomenon was at its height, many of us wondered, 'Why do people have to go to Toronto to experience this blessing? Or Holy Trinity Brompton? Or Queen's Road in Wimbledon?' When someone asked me these questions I answered, 'And what if we *do* have to go to one of those places? Will we do it?'

You may not have lost your anointing at Toronto or Queen's Road or HTB, but you *may* have to go there – or wherever God is powerfully at work – to find God's special presence once again. Would you be willing to do this? If that is where God is at work, will you and I have the humility and integrity to go there – and be utterly open – to rediscover God's special presence?

We may say, 'God can meet with me in the privacy of my own place of prayer.' No doubt. He certainly can. But it is my experience that God tests me to the hilt – to see how much I want him – by not coming to me in power until I seek him with all my heart wherever he may be at work. When Naaman the leper was told to seek out Elisha the prophet he might have said, 'Let him come to me.' Even after he did go to Elisha's house and was given ridiculous advice – 'Go, wash yourself seven times in the Jordan' (2 Kgs. 5:10) – Naaman reasoned that the rivers in his own land were 'better than any of the waters of Israel' (2 Kgs. 5:12). But he was not healed until he went to the place God had chosen to work.

> 'For my thoughts are not your thoughts, neither are your ways my ways,' declares the LORD. (Isa. 55:8)

> But God chose the foolish things of the world to shame the wise; God chose the weak things of the world to shame the strong. He chose the lowly things of this world and the despised things – and the things that are not – to nullify the things that are, so that no one may boast before him. (1 Cor. 1:27–9)

Having to accept a different anointing from what we lost

A return *to* the anointing, not a return *of* the anointing, means that God will decide how to fill our emptiness. We may well reason that the only sense of God we will accept is the way we have always known him. But he may choose to let that wait for a while – perhaps indefinitely. As I said, this Jesus Joseph and Mary saw was truly their son but not an aspect of him they knew so well. This Jesus would never be quite the same to them again.

In my own return to Jerusalem, this is one of the hardest things I have had to face. To this very day I have not experienced that exact same sense of God – when Jesus was more real to me than anybody else – I once knew. But he has been pleased to show himself to me equally power-fully – indeed, more so, but in a different way. I still long for what I had. But at the same time I do not question for a moment that what I have found is the same Jesus I previously experienced!

Early in my ministry at the Chapel, when those visits with Dr Lloyd-Jones gave me a hunger for the old intimacy with the Lord, I assumed that the same exact feeling would immediately return to me if I quickly put my house in order. I admit to 'tokens' and 'tastes' now and then, but so far it is *not* what I once felt. And yet, for all I know, God probably works through me today in a way he could not have done then. I have had to be content with a different anointing – one that is maintained by a continual spirit of dignifying trials and totally forgiving others – from the anointing that once came on me unexpectedly without my turning my hand. I only know that I would not ex-change anything in this world for what I now have. And if I am totally honest, I prefer what I now have to what I previously lost; but I do not deny I'd love to have the same old feeling as well.

Being willing to accept an anointing that is different from what we may specifically expect or seek

Once we have lost the special presence of the Dove, whether it be by our grieving him or because God sovereignly 'stayed behind' as we moved on, we forfeit any 'right' to demand the return of the same anointing. We therefore must be willing to adjust to the way God chooses to manifest his glory should he be gracious to do so.

Joseph and Mary were desperate. Upset though they were when they found their son showing his glory in an unexpected way, they were in no way going to walk away from him!

You may have been seeking the Lord but not with the openness to the Spirit that you thought was required. By 'openness' I mean taking God any way you find him, seeking him with all your heart and being willing to adjust to any aspect or measure of his glory he is willing to unveil.

The forgotten anointing also consists of those hidden ways God can speak and act which nobody has yet experienced. What if God were to show up to *you* in a way he hadn't done to those you respected most? What if he shows up in your life in a way he didn't do with Athanasias, Luther, Calvin, Wesley or your present hero? Will you still welcome him?

When the psalmist speaks of God confiding in those who fear him – which the Authorized Version terms 'the secret of the LORD' (Ps. 25:14), you must expect the Lord to tell you anything! You may also be required to keep quiet about it! This is why it is a secret – and why he confides.

He may have in mind a special relationship with you that nobody else on earth has. Were that to be the case, you can be quite certain you will be required to keep it to yourself until you get to Heaven. If you say, 'That wouldn't be fun if I couldn't tell it,' you can also be sure this privilege will not be offered.

God is seeking those who seek him with such openness that he can be himself to that person in a way he cannot be to others. He is a jealous God and looks for someone who is happy for God to be the only person who knows what is happening to them (see again John 5:44). This means a willingness to accept an anointing that is different from what you expect or seek.

Accepting his gentle rebuke when he is found

Jesus' response to his parents was, 'Didn't you know I had to be in my Father's house?' (Luke 2:49). As Calvin put it, 'Christ is right to reprove his mother, though he does so with restraint and indirectly.' Jesus would not break a bruised reed (Matt. 12:20). Both Joseph and Mary were bruised reeds by this time. They needed a rebuke, but how gentle it was!

When we return to the anointing we may expect a rebuke. But it is always tender. Job's words, 'How faint the whisper' (Job 26:14), perfectly describe the way God often speaks. The Holy Spirit's sensitivity to us results in tremendous peace and calm when we are sensitive to him. It is not unlike Elijah's discovering a new way God manifested himself: not in the wind, the earthquake or fire but 'a gentle whisper' (1 Kgs. 19:12). It is the way you and I are advised to approach another person who has been overtaken in a sin (Gal. 6:1). When we are harsh and judgmental, we are not mirroring the Spirit of Jesus.

The unveiling of God's glory is usually characterised by a rebuke, exposure of some weakness or sin. This is how we grow. I have talked to many people (and hear of many others) who learned lessons from the Lord 'on the floor' when they fell after being prayed for. My wife Louise is a good example. She phoned me from Florida in January 1995 while at the meetings conducted by Rodney Howard-Browne. 'It is the greatest thing that has ever happened to me, the nearest you get to Heaven without dying.' She spent hours on the carpet – listening to and *learning* from the Lord. Her chief concern when she came back to London was: 'I don't want to lose this.' It has changed her life.

A return to the anointing, then, will almost certainly mean hearing something from God that amounts to a rebuke. Why? We all need to change. Joseph and Mary needed to change.

Accepting truth we may not wish were true

When Jesus asked, 'Didn't you know I had to be in my Father's house?' he was lovingly confronting his parents with the truth they didn't want to hear. And yet, as Calvin put it, 'The wonder is that Joseph and Mary did not understand this reply.' They knew better than anybody the truth about Jesus.

The unfolding of God's glory is also the unfolding of truth. This may mean truth we hadn't wanted fully to accept – at least not yet.

This can be exceedingly difficult for those in leadership, especially if we have espoused teaching that we may have to abandon. It is harder if we have to accept teaching we had opposed, and harder still if we have gone to print – and have to retract! I have had to do so, but the inner peace and joy far outweigh the fear of criticism which may or may not follow. Sadly, I know some people who wouldn't change *because* they were committed to print. If this unwillingness to change is in the face of clear biblical teaching, I would fear becoming yesterday's man overnight – like King Saul.

Jesus said, 'If anyone chooses to do God's will, he will find out whether my teaching comes from God or whether I speak on my own' (John 7:17). That means if I am obedient I will come to truth and can be preserved from grievous error. But if that truth is right there before my eyes but I can't bear the thought of embracing it, my prayer for an ever-increasing anointing is not sincere.

There are thousands of doctrines taught by Christians which often contradict each other. This can only mean they aren't all correct and somebody at some time moved ahead without Jesus and took a following with them. I am not so naïve as to believe that all of us who desire a greater anointing will be able to sign our names to each other's theology. We must be true to ourselves. But at the same time it is surely not good that some Christians can oppose each other on some of the most fundamental teachings of God's word.

Being put in our place

That is exactly what happened to Joseph and Mary, and all of us can expect this to happen to us when we rediscover the special presence of God. Why? Well, to keep us from taking ourselves too seriously.

Joseph and Mary not only focused on themselves but also felt that God owed them something. Rather than being thrilled that they found Jesus, they were angry. They possibly felt betrayed. They now took it personally that Jesus was perfectly at home in the temple courts with the teachers of the Law and not with them. They didn't want God to be God; they wanted to maintain control.

The return to the anointing means a total surrender of control. This means we affirm God's own opinion. Whereas we may in one sense rightly refer to *our* anointing, at the end of the day it is not ours – it is his. It is 'on loan', as it were. We must therefore respect it and never forget that we can lose it again. We lose it when we try to control.

Joseph and Mary had lost control and now they wanted it back. But Jesus' question, 'Didn't you know I had to be in my Father's house?' helped them accept their place.

> Do not be quick with your mouth,
>   do not be hasty in your heart
>   to utter anything before God.
> God is in heaven
>   and you are on earth,
>   so let your words be few. (Eccles. 5:2)

I reckon that Jesus' soft question to his parents was in private. Luke does not specifically say this but it seems likely that Jesus put this to them when the three of them went off to one side. Not only does Jesus not break a bruised reed but he also has a way of letting us save face. There may be exceptions, but generally speaking God does not tend to put us in our place by embarrassing us before people looking on, but kindly teaches us a lesson we will never forget by showing us our folly in secret. Even when the public proclamation of the word exposes any of us, no one but God really knows what is taking place inside our hearts.

Not understanding the obvious at first

'But they did not understand what he was saying to them' (Luke 2:50). They should have, but they didn't. A return to the anointing will bring us face to face with things we cannot fully grasp partly because, even if we should have, we have not seen all of the implications of what we have once been taught. As we have seen, Joseph and Mary knew more than anybody the truth as to Jesus' origin. But they still didn't catch on when he referred to having to be in his Father's house. Joseph should have known that Jesus wasn't referring to him but to God the Father.

Jesus' style of asking questions years later was not entirely unlike his question to Joseph and Mary. He had a way of asking a question that might have tended to make one feel a bit stupid – but it was always done to rebuke unbelief. For example, when Jesus enabled Peter to walk on the water all went well until Peter saw the wind. He cried out to be saved as he began to sink. 'Immediately Jesus reached out his hand and caught him. "You of little faith," he said, *"why did you doubt?"* ' (Matt. 14:31). On another occasion, when asked about the parable of the sower, Jesus said to his disciples, 'Don't you understand *this* parable?' as if saying, 'This is an easy one,' for he added, 'How then will you understand any parable?' (Mark 4:13). He did not really do this to make them feel stupid but to force them to look again at what he had just said and conclude for themselves what he felt was obvious.

So too with any manifestation of God's glory. At first our reaction may be bewilderment. But looking again in the light of what we have already learned will reveal that there is a credible explanation for what God chooses to do.

Focusing on Christ's glory

The ultimate reason for the return to the anointing – and any manifestation of God's glory – is that God will be the main attraction. That was the permanent lesson in this story of Joseph and Mary finding Jesus in the temple. He held centre stage! They did not seem ready for this.

> I am the LORD; that is my name!
> I will not give my glory to another. (Isa. 42:8)

I suspect that all delays to seeing God's glory manifested are partly explained by an unconscious desire in us to have a share of the glory in what God does. I doubt there is such a thing as an unmixed motive. We may tell ourselves that our prayer for Revival is entirely for God's honour. We may feel the same way over wanting a greater anointing, that it is only for *his* sake. We may think we truly mean that.

But one thing is certain: when and where God does show up he will come in such a manner that no sane person will think it is because of what he or she did for God. It will be God turning up in such a way that he gets the total credit. 'It is not for your sake, O house of Israel, that I am going to do these things, but for the sake of my holy name' (Ezek. 36:22). The moment any of us elbows in on God's territory one of two things will follow: either he will back off entirely, or we will be removed from the picture. 'So that no one may boast before him' (1 Cor. 1:29).

God is sensitive about his own honour and the Holy Spirit mirrors that sensitivity. Adjustment to him means our forfeiting any control or credit in order that he remain in our midst – as the Dove remained on Jesus.

Conclusion

Then he went down to Nazareth with them and was obedient
to them. But his mother treasured all these things in her heart.
(Luke 2:51)

Do you believe that you are consciously in the will of God?
God wants us to be in his will and to know what his will is.
For Paul exhorted us to 'understand what the Lord's will is'
(Eph. 5:17). This word followed the previous admonition
'Find out what pleases the Lord' (Eph. 5:10). When we find
out what pleases the Lord – and then do what pleases him
– we may be sure that we are in his will.

The inner testimony of the Spirit, which will always
correspond to God's revealed will (the Bible), is sufficient
to convey that we are in his will. If we are not in his will it
is either because we didn't obey God's explicit word, like
Jonah (Jonah 1:1–3), or because we moved ahead of him,
like Joseph and Mary.

But 'all's well that ends well', as Shakespeare put it. In the
case of Jonah, God came to him a second time and he
obeyed (Jonah 3:1–3). And at the end of the day, after having
had a quarrel with the Lord, Jonah let God have the last

word (Jonah 4:11). All ended well for Samson too; he accomplished more at the end of his life 'than while he lived' (Judg. 16:30).

And so it was with Joseph and Mary. All three of the above accounts have these ingredients in common: the people referred to were temporarily out of God's will but fully in it in the end. Is it possible to be out of the will of God and yet in the will of God at the same time? Yes. God permits things in our lives which get us off the rails for a while but nonetheless are in the purpose of his long-term strategy. All that is permitted as to time and circumstance is redeemable. In other words, God helps us to buy back time, as it were; he repays us for the years the locusts have eaten (Joel 2:25). 'And we know that all things work together for good to them that love God, to them who are called according to his purpose' (Rom. 8:28 AV).

Samson developed a sensitivity to the Spirit during the time 'the hair on his head began to grow after it had been shaved' (Judg. 16:22). Whether one has sinned grievously like Samson, or runs ahead of the Lord like Joseph and Mary, God does not desert his own. His aim in any case is to teach us his 'ways' – if we will listen. As long as we can hear God's voice and accept his rebukes it means we are not stone deaf to the Spirit. Not only is God not finished with us but the best is around the corner.

Knowing God's 'ways' comes from developing an ever-increasing sensitivity to his Spirit. This is what we are all invited to and it is a most gracious invitation. Never turn down an opportunity like this!

Joseph and Mary made the adjustment to Jesus and their relationship thereafter was richer than ever. For one thing, you can be sure they had a respect for the Son of God that was probably somewhat taken for granted before. Once we return to the anointing we have a reverence and appreciation for it which helps ensure we don't repeat past mistakes.

We can learn from Jesus' example too. He submitted to his parents in accordance with the Law (Exod. 20:12) and his mission to fulfil it (Matt. 5:17). His obedience was an act of humility for our salvation. 'He fulfilled God's intentions,' says Calvin, 'that for a time he should shelter under Joseph's name, as under a shadow. . . All the more freely should we, each of us, undergo the yoke which the Lord may lay upon our necks.'

Thus Jesus was sensitive to the Spirit when he stayed behind in Jerusalem and continued to be sensitive to the Spirit by submitting to his parents. What was true in his life and ministry years later – he 'did not please himself' (Rom. 15:3) – had now begun in earnest. All sensitivity to the Spirit, of which Jesus was the supreme example, consists in our not pleasing ourselves.

The yoke which the Lord may lay upon our necks, therefore, is to be welcomed. It is the best way to live. Jesus invited us to learn from him that we may find rest for our souls. For his yoke is easy and his burden is light (Matt. 11:29–30).

May the blessing of God Almighty be upon you.

Notes

1 Although doves and pigeons are in the same order of birds scientifically, there seem to be no empirical studies available on their temperaments. The focus of scientific investigation centres mainly on their origins, locations, sizes, colour and feeding habits.

2 The so-called 'London pigeons' in Trafalgar Square, like the pigeons which flock in every city centre, are called 'feral' pigeons.

3 *Peristera* is the Greek word for dove, *trygon* for turtle-dove. Many theologians relate the reference to the turtle-dove in Song of Songs 2:12 to the Holy Spirit. The ancient Hebrew scholar Philo saw the dove as a symbol of the *logos* (word), the *nous* (mind) or *sophia* (wisdom). The NIV translation of Song of Songs 2:12 ('the cooing of the dove') does not reflect that turtle-dove in fact is meant in the original language. And yet the general word for dove may well imply turtle-dove in most cases in either the Old or New Testament, even if the specific word for turtle-dove is not used.

4 A monastery in Syria where Aramaic is spoken exists today. It is claimed there that Jesus taught Aramaic to

the people during the period of his life before he was thirty.

5 From 'To a Louse, on Seeing One on a Lady's Bonnet at Church'. The pompous lady did not know that everybody but she could see the head lice she had.

6 This is the name given by the *Sunday Telegraph* when describing the phenomenon of falling down and laughing, either after being prayed for or through the laying on of hands. I initially had grave doubts but eventually accepted it as a genuine move of the Spirit. I have been understandably criticised for my stand, as many thought it would lead me away from my ministry of expository preaching. We did lose twenty members and no doubt several more who regularly attended Westminster Chapel. It made me sensitive to my critics who felt that the Toronto Blessing would replace the importance of preaching.

7 Speaking generally, a Calvinist believes in predestination and the eternal security of the believer. See my *Calvin and English Calvinism to 1649* (Paternoster).